Owls Head Revisited

Jim Krosschell

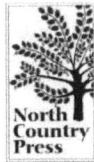

North Country Press

Owls Head Revisited

ISBN 978-1-943424-02-3

Library of Congress Control Number 2015941535

North Country Press
Unity, Maine

To Cindy, Kate, and Emma

Acknowledgments

I'd like to thank several journals for publishing parts of this book, in somewhat different forms.

Introduction, "Owls Head Revisited," in *Waccamaw Review* 8: 2011

Chapter 3, "Ingraham's Hill," in *The Leopard Seal*, 1:1, 2014

Chapter 7, "Islands and Points," in *Words and Images*, Spring 2014

Chapter 9, "Marshes," a section published as "Walmart on the Weskeag" in *Wilderness House Review*, 8:3, 2013

Introduction

The town of Owl's Head, Maine, occupies a peninsula on the west side of Penobscot Bay, a town in little more than name, for there is almost no business to patronize, and not much development to rue, yet, and its civil governance dances calmly to the once-a-year warrants of the August town meeting. Our inhabitants fish, or commute to Rockland, or dabble in retirement, or keep the summer people in lobster and workable plumbing. The place is ordinary – small white houses, scruffy woodlots, half-mown fields, perpetual yard sales; and dramatic – mansions on the shore, stunning views of the bay and its islands and the open ocean between Vinalhaven and Spruce Head. For some, it's a home; for others like me, it's been a second home, a refuge from the city and its ambitious trials.

Every day now I walk one of three routes, each ending at the water: a beach, a point, a cove. In my little neighborhood of comfort, I'm the guy that waves at every passing car, the guy from away who sometimes has his little black poodle and sometimes not. Whatever the drivers – of pickups, rust buckets, Beamers from Connecticut – think of this, they almost always wave back.

That's one of the things I like about Owl's Head. Another is that its biggest controversies, now that the airport is firmly entrenched, seem to be orthographic. How do you spell the town's name, for example? Half of the sign makers and journalists around here, being either careless or ornery, exclude the apostrophe. The other half include it, following the rules of metaphor and history (not to mention grammar), for the high promontory upon which the lighthouse sits is said to look like an owl in profile, and the old Abenaki name

Mecadacut means owl's head. Omitting the apostrophe makes little sense, as if one head could have many owls. But it could be worse: Owlshead, anyone?

Similarly and perhaps more colorfully, the archipelago of islands just off its shores – Otter, High, Dix, Pleasant and the rest – is a Ridge known prosaically as Mussel and poetically as Muscle. I know of no municipal preference between the homonyms, although the one word is clearly derived from the other. I will revisit these islands later.

According to the guide books, the town has two and a half attractions, of which my wife and I have visited one. Always heading the lists is the Owl's Head Transportation Museum, semi-famous among antique car nuts; along with the half-attraction, Knox County Regional Airport, it forms an unholy alliance of air shows on summer weekends. The second, Owl's Head Light, is semi-famous among lighthouse nuts, and there we do take visitors, walking along sheer cliffs and past the white keeper's house from 1854, climbing the steps of the promontory and tower (open only a couple of times a week, in summer), stepping into the lantern room 100 feet above the bay, into the glorious view of the islands and Rockland Harbor and the Camden Hills rising in the north. Our visitor's tour also includes Birch Point Beach State Park for Maine's iconic tide pools and sand and pink granite ledges, and Owl's Head Harbor to see the small fleet of lobster boats and the ratty, smelly town wharf. The tour lasts little more than an hour before giving way to drinks on the deck.

Metaphorically and naturally, Owl's Head is a quiet town, so un-ambitious that the library is open but an hour on Wednesday evening ("weather permitting") and two hours on Saturday afternoon. The built environment, however, isn't particularly so, with the whining of Maine's official insect, the chain saw, and the buzzing of riding mowers on large lawns, and the throaty rumble of lobster boats in the bay, and (my own enduring nemesis) the snarling of airplanes – pleasure props, mail flights serving Matinicus, Embraers commuting from Boston, air-show antiques, and the occasional rich man's Gulfstream – coming in too low and too loud. But these interruptions are flare-ups, not the insistent and perpetual insults of a city, and for the most part Owl's Head lives peacefully on the tax revenue from the summer people on its shores.

****

For most of my life, ever since a boyhood trip to visit my uncle-professor in Brunswick, Maine has been a vision of simplicity and escape and idyllic joy, a kind of Arcadia. In the 16th century, Verrazano actually called it so, after the wilderness in Greece, referring not only to Maine but to the whole Atlantic seaboard from Virginia to Labrador. American Arcadia didn't last long. Samuel de Champlain (first European explorer of Owl's Head in 1605) dropped the "r" (was it too hard to pronounce? For a Frenchman?), and the marketing of Acadia and the parade of wars – territorial, religious, symbolic – was on. The British and French and Dutch and Spanish and Abenaki exchanged bullets for 150 years over the bounties of land and shore. Revolutionary America hastened the process, industrial America completed the rout. The siren romance of Acadia had led to its destruction, and the wilderness, the purity, clings barely to life today, institutionalized in a national park on Mt. Desert Island, under attack in the Great North Woods, fictionalized in my mind.

I know that for many people, Owl's Head is no Acadia. The fog here is legendary – our personal current record is eight straight July days shut of sun and ocean; not enough acres of land are conserved and protected from future malls or mansions; the airport is right in the middle of everything, a reminder of business travel and tourists from away; too many people are poor; the winter is long and cold and two-thirds dark. Yet my family and I have come eagerly for nearly 20 years, just escaping the city perhaps, or caught in an illusion of Acadia. Until retirement, we came wearing our Massachusetts straitjackets of performance and calculations and tyrannical schedules of work and school. Those few weeks of vacation and the occasional holiday weekend were enough to loosen the straps but not cast them off. Our visits here were always too short, not enough for healing of stress, not enough to escape into, or create, an ideal world. The mountaintop could be seen but not reached. The suburban life sets the mind on a narrow path, and the body dutifully climbs along, hoping for clear views before the fall of night turns it back.

The very words "visit" and "revisit" suggest a stopover ruled by the clock in blocks of time. But I'm not visiting anymore, and I'm not technically revisiting either. In retirement, my focus is different. I'm in Owl's Head much more often than I used to be. Time is changing from a construct to a dimension, from a jolting digital read-out to a long morning dawn. It is on my side, at least for a while. After a stay here I no longer leave with eyes wide shut, desperately reviewing the calendar for the next fix, pulled back by a whim or an obsession. I'm embarking on a different kind of revisitation, a twitch upon the thread of the ordinary, hoping to see, really for the first time, Ballyhac Cove and Ingraham Hill and the ghostly, long-gone ash trees of Ash Point. And I will be walking, not driving; observing, not glancing; giving, not accumulating; believing, not escaping.

And my language is changing, too. During those 40 years of dreaming of a different life, my idea was to escape corporations and society by writing fiction on the side, as if writing fiction would ease stress and distress. But a different language has slowly emerged, and what I worried was just a dream is becoming much less so.

****

The capturing in words of a story, a feeling, a character, an image, even a philosophy is an activity out of time, wrested away from time. Time is lost track of. You don't have to follow its rules until you get tired.

I could also say, equally, that writing for me, fiction or essays, seems to require a place where time and space are compatible, or even congruent, where the landscape and our presence in it reflect any number of eras. Maine is that kind of place. I sit on the town wharf, looking out at boats and islands and horizon, and it could be the 16th century, or the 21st, so little beyond the shore has changed. It is a place where the restless are quieted by the ordinary. But it's also a place where I've discovered I don't need fiction, to write or to read, as desperately as I used to. I can experience the contradictions and pleasures of life more directly.

And Owl's Head is a place of both, a place where I understand the centuries-old *memento mori* "Et in Arcadia ego" in both its interpretations. In the frazzled city I am the speaker: "Even though I'm dead, I still had Arcadia," and I think about some new plot or life or character twist to bring me back there. In Owl's Head death is the speaker: "Even in Arcadia I exist," and I think about the real systems of nature all around: the trillions of births in the tidal zone, the natural deaths of trees. Kids grown, job retired, I'm learning this lesson of contradictions, studying the sentence of death, coming to grips with something previously sublimated by work or fiction. Commutation of the sentence won't be possible, they tell me, but at least I'm not going to make up my life anymore, I'm going to parse it by a gull standing firm in a gale, a fog creeping over the islands, a lane leading nowhere, a stew of molecules recombining in the sea.

Some people, not to mention writers of fiction, try to mend life by unifying the sacred and the profane. But for the irreligious, that marriage is only possible if we are given the time to be out of time. We have to shake off the world, and yet inhabit it completely. There is no escaping it, especially since I believe there is no other world but this one, and therefore sacred must take on a different meaning. I have to reject the Gnostic imprisonment of mystery. Waugh in *Brideshead Revisited* couldn't, or at least his characters wouldn't let him. My memories and work here have little to do with the obsessive kind of belief in love or God pursued by the restless, the inconstant. Fictional worlds are wonderful for rests after lunch, for plane rides, for pews, for the quiet half-hours just before, and after, sleep. In a place like Owl's Head, love is a chance to fit in with the world, not fight against it. And religion is a goldfinch singing at the very top of a balsam fir, tiny and defiant; it is the bay shining in a rainbow of colors far beyond blue if you stare yourself open to them; it is the melting and draining of ego.

Now I have time to become whole. Writing is my revisitation. Writing becomes a guide to inner creation, not outer complicity. The day reduces to simplicity: mornings spent clearing the body in the words of the mind, afternoons spent clearing the mind in the sweat of the body. Owl's Head opens up in a symphony of the ordinary, walking a lane, listening to surf, splitting wood for the stove, tending lawn and garden, doing nothing for an hour but watching birds flying over the bay and between the firs. How many of us are so lucky as to get four or five stabs of pure joy in the course of one day? Even while weeding? And then writing it down, or trying to: the best kind of revisitation.

This is the place where, oddly enough and increasingly so, the pursuit of that old material life – based on flights of money and ambition and purchase of the latest this and that – is what seems abstract. This is the place where a lobsterman pulls up to the wharf, weighs his catch, and knows exactly how much he's earned for the day's labors. This is where a flight of fancy becomes a walk on the shore, where words have more weight.

I'm emboldened now to take up the contradictions of life, questions of good and evil, the co-existence of death and breath, the finality of the heartbeat, the darkness of winter light. But am I still a visitor, with restless city ways? Is there time and energy enough? How to be still after years of knee-jiggling in offices and airplanes, how to disentangle from the Web of distraction, how to love fog and cold and loneliness, how to persevere – well, these are fairly ridiculous questions, themselves driven by the skepticism of a lifetime. Let me put them aside for a moment and at the very least, and with no little glee, drop the apostrophe of good sense, embrace illogic, poetry, bulging muscles and multiple heads, and trust that Owls Head is a place where I can inhabit them all.

****

This book is therefore a new inhabitation, not a history, of Owls Head. There are a few facts here, to be sure, dates and people and events I've gathered from real history books and from two books about the town. The first is a book of old photographs collected by a fellow tourist in residence. Edward Wayman Coffin self-published *The Coastal Town of Owls Head, Maine* in 2004. The photos in his book, supplemented by words, show families and houses and boats, and they are meaningful perhaps to the Crocketts and Haskells and Packards and Heards who descended from the settlers streaming in after the Revolutionary War, but I can't imagine to many others. I for one am after a picture both bigger and smaller, more universal and more ordinary. Photos won't do – their connections seem two-dimensional at best, trapped. I want the other dimensions, the depth, time, emotions and aspirations that words carry along, echoing out of ancient bedrock and deep seas, lost loves and black crows, and the patient, long-suffering pointed firs braving the shore.

A second book about this town, *Owls Head*, by the photographic artist Rosamond Purcell, was published in 2003. It too has photos (and forsakes the apostrophe) but only a few, carefully chosen to show man-made objects in decay, jumbled and rotting and ghostly in a huge salvage/junk/antiques yard in the village, sometimes pictured in situ, sometimes purchased and transported to her studio in Boston and arranged for the camera. Purcell addresses the yard's owner and his biography, but her meditations on man-made stuff say very little about Maine and almost nothing about the natural world. Indeed, William Buckminster, the owner, could have been an eccentric in almost any small town in America if I hadn't seen his place for myself. To each his own obsessions: mine are concerned with the whole of the life cycle, not just its manufactured offshoots, not just the end of items.

To get at what I want and feel, I have undertaken a kind of walking tour of Owls Head. It's not a big place, just 9 square miles of land. (I won't walk the 11 square miles of ocean!) In effect, it consists of two peninsulas, one to the east, one to the south, plus a bit of Rockland suburb to the north and the airport in the west and some no-man's land scattered here and there. On *The Maine Atlas and Gazetteer*, my Bible and inspiration, the obvious, touristy part of town is the peninsula that juts northeast-ward into Penobscot Bay, ending in the lighthouse that marks the bay's southern end. We'll get to that in due course. I'm going to start my tour with the other peninsula, which is a peninsula only in a squashed, pug-faced kind of way. It points south like almost every other good peninsula in Maine, but unlike them is not long and narrow with a numbered state road traversing its length to lands-end. Its southern side is much wider than its western (Ballyhac Cove) and eastern (Atlantic Ocean) sides, and on the atlas it looks as if it took an uppercut from a big-city bully. This pseudo-peninsula divides into two neighborhoods (I use the term loosely – Owls Head has no real neighborhoods as a city person would know them), Ash Point on the east, where I live and where this clockwise tour will end, and Ballyhac on the west, where the tour starts. It will be a walking tour on land even though Owls Head was settled for the bounties of the sea. This landlubber loves and needs the ocean for its dreamy shores, not its boating adventures.

And so, guided by a large map left by the previous owners of our house, a map hand-drawn in 1978 and mimeographed for the Owls Head Fire Department, I've walked every foot of every road over the course of a year – seventeen different excursions starting June 30, 2011 and ending August 7, 2012, and not just on nice summer days either. I've seen as much shoreline as I was allowed, trespassed on as many driveways as I dared, tramped through woods and fields without getting shot, imagined histories of fox and farmer, lobster and fisherman, got lost in a field of lupine and a strand of kelp, got Lyme disease. I'd explore with a notebook and return brimming with ideas to be captured, to be slept on, to be developed into a chapter. Then I'd write until it was time for the next adventure.

Since that last purposeful walk, I've been visiting and revisiting, writing and revising, pontificating and apologizing for pontificating, of course still walking every day, trying to meet a few people as well as deer, becoming humbled, perhaps even becoming balanced.

Walk with me, then, as I outline the natural and human neighborhoods of a little town in Maine.

Table of Contents

The house rests on a rise that slopes down to the ocean a quarter mile away. It has a long view out to sea that is rare for this part of Maine, obstructed by no trees or hills. But there's no one in the house to see it, and hasn't been for a long time: windows broken, roof shingles missing, cedar shakes gray and curling, walls listing. The house has resisted weather and progress, sited in a kind of anomalous tableau that is fuzzy in origin and retrograde of time. The land was cleared but the trees never grew back; a stony field on one side of the road and a grassy marsh on the other have settled on the downhill slopes; the remnants of a fishing village on the shore hint at a way of life hundreds of years old. The whole environs looks lost, a remnant of old sainted Maine, a hidden pocket oddly neglected, a place as lush and stark as anything in Washington County way Down East. I don't understand how it stays free of the developers.

Like empty shore lots, abandoned houses of the old style are rare in mid-coast Maine. They usually succumb to the bulldozer, the mansion-maker, the pilferer of old boards, or even the endowment of a museum. Those that are left feed dreams. I imagine this was a saltwater farm in the 19th century, even the 18th, with some land cleared for grazing and some set aside for haying and some kept in trees for firewood, a kitchen garden for a front yard, venison in the forest, cod in the ocean, and a dory at anchor from which to catch supper or a little cash down at the Owls Head wharf. The family lived simply. It was a harsh life undoubtedly, especially in winter, but a self-sufficient one, and one in which the pleasures of eating and sheltering and simple family entertainment sprang immediately out of the land and the sea, and worries and troubles came directly, bold as a southeaster, not filtered by brokerage statements or television news or instant messages from children far away. They dreamed also of heaven, I expect, but I'd like to believe they reserved salvation for the end of life, not for the vividness of its duration. A saltwater farm compels attention. And so we dream locally, these mythical farmers and I, of place, nature, or family, instead of big houses and fancy clothes in some world removed from the shore. In this part of Maine the view is still backwards.

Yet the reality is most likely that the people were driven, or lured, away. Florida's warm beaches prevailed against the long dark winters, or the price of fish plummeted when the factory ships started to vacuum the sea, or shoreline taxes became unbearable, and all the while images of city comfort, anonymity, the wealth of money seeped into souls. Children always leave the nest; what has changed in most of Maine is that they seldom come back.

Ah, the chance not to leave. Would the richness of nature have been enough for the likes of me? Logically, it's impossible to have nostalgia for something I never had, for work I wouldn't be suited for, for a place I too, in my ambition, probably would have left. In that simpler way of life, there would have been few intellectual opportunities, and no way to slake the wanderlust I'd gathered from books. But what have I gained in the American Diaspora? I too have been terribly seduced.

That Maine family is long gone to glory, their shore land sold to summercators, but somehow this house at the end of Makers Cove Road hangs on. Increasingly in Maine, especially coastal Maine, one has to look hard for such remnants of a dream revisited. One of the reasons that Andrew Wyeth's painting "Christina's World" is so evocative is that the Olsen House, already more than 150 years old when he painted it in 1948, is frozen in the middle of its long, gentle erosion into night. You greet generations of ghosts – owners, boarders, artists, tourists – and mingle with them on the shrine's grounds, their ordinary lives made public and conquering time.

But as I walk farther, past the house, I see signs of the new kind of erosion. Fishing may be a losing cause, farming these days becomes boutique and depends on tourists in farmers' markets and upscale restaurants, so what happens to the land where those families used to live? What do owners do? The wealthy ones (mostly from away) can afford to keep oceanfront lots for themselves even considering the way towns tax them. They might even deed the land back to nature, to be preserved in trusts and parks. But the few remaining owners of average means have no such choices. They must sell their lots, or develop them for people whose livelihoods come from elsewhere.

And so, amidst fish shacks and a couple of run-down cottages, one house on the shore is being renovated, and another just starting the process, with new siding and new roofs and additions in which to watch television. These are not big-city developers, judging by the lack of monster windows and instant lawns, but new or newly inspired owners seeking some comfort and profit. Still, the wave seems to be coming, spilling over from the more suburban shores of Ash Point and Holiday Beach just a couple of miles away, from the airport, from the big-box stores and tourist traffic blaring in Rockland. How long before this place too is crawling with SUVs and For Sale signs? Bold Atlantic Coast! Country Peace and Quiet! Minutes from All Conveniences! At least for now, and generally so along Ballyhac's quiet coves and wooded lanes and the protected land of Birch Point Beach State Park, the 21st century is making only the slightest of impacts.

****

The Maine Atlas and Gazetteer is divided into 70 squares, running from map #1 featuring outlet-heaven Kittery in the far south, to #70 in the far northwest featuring a gloriously absolute nothing. Every time I pick up the atlas to fantasize about Mt. Katahdin, or check a place name from the past, or just transcend the present, I'm amazed at the #8 of Owls Head. Like other low numbers – Kennebunk (#3), Portland (#3 and #5), and Brunswick (#6) – we should have developed into northern Massachusetts by now. But we haven't.

Ballyhac, the least developed section of Owls Head with a name, occupies its southwestern part. On the east, several hundred acres of road-less woods separate it from Ash Point, Ballyhac Cove separates it from South Thomaston on the west, and the waters of Muscle Ridge Channel on the south separate it from the rest of the world. Ballyhac Road itself starts at the airport and winds down about a mile and a half south to the water, spawning a few minor lanes near its beginning, and then three other bigger roads branching off half-way down, Makers Cove Road and Dyer Point Road and State Park Road. In 1978, the date of my Fire Department map, Ballyhac Road was called Park Road, the only one of the whole neighborhood with a name.

This summer I've taken several walks down the roads of Ballyhac. One begins on a warm morning when I park the car at the north end of Ballyhac Road, near the airport. I've driven this road many times, taking the kids and visitors to the state park, but never walked it. It could be anywhere in rural Maine. The woods are a bit scraggly, full of alders and young birch. Few big pines have grown back from centuries of logging. The land looks damp. The lawns of small white houses are cluttered with junk, like perpetual yard sales. Roberts Lane leads to a large house, with manicured lawn, set back into trees, and the sheds of an excavation company behind the house. Fathom Lane, another glorified driveway, displays fine white gravel, like a sport wearing spats, and ends in a center-entrance Colonial, needing paint but still weirdly suburban. On Meadowbrook Lane four ramshackle houses decay not just from weather and time but from the sheer poverty of their inhabitants. The proximity of the airport clearly makes property affordable here for working families trying to squeeze a living from the land and the culture, as they've been doing for centuries in Maine, plowing roads and chopping wood and serving as stern men and taking in small appliances or sewing or children in daycare.

Just before the evidence of this protean, slightly desperate way of life starts to change, where Ballyhac Road meets the bigger houses of Makers Cove Road, I'm drawn out of analysis and into nightmare. I almost miss the shrine as I walk by, and certainly would have missed it in a car. A short path leads to a wooden box set on the ground under trees. The front of the box is glassed in as if displaying icons in a church. Inside are faded photos – a young man and woman, the young man kissing a baby – and cards and papers such as a printed funeral program titled Journey's End Lane, and a simple tacked-on paper banner hand-written with "Brandon, June 13, 1986." No cause or means of death is given, no last name. I can only assume that the date is his birthday, not death day, unless this place has mourned him for 25 years. And who is Brandon? A murdered man? A SIDS baby? The stark uncertainty is haunting.

Private grief is rarely made so public in Maine.

I might try opening the door of the box. There might be an explanation somewhere inside, like a placard in a museum. But that would feel like opening a coffin, and even though the houseplant decorating the top of the box is mostly dried and dead, and the path almost overgrown, as if visitors come here seldom, say, only on June 13, I feel I would be discovered as soon as I touched the glass. Someone would drive up, stop, and unsmilingly look at me like an intruder, an out-of-stater poorly equipped to understand such a direct tragedy. I cannot interpret Brandon's world; Wyeth might have.

Just past the shrine is Journey's End Lane itself. Brandon must have lived down here. Can I re-create him by seeing his house, or by a chance meeting with wife or mother? A mailbox and stone marked #1 come first, but the driveway winds into the woods out of sight, silently shouting private property. The rest of the lane is just as unrevealing: it starts with an ungainly house on a large lot completely devoid of trees and shrubs, surrounded by grass mowed down to a half-inch, like a modern Olsen House keeping the wilderness at bay; it proceeds for a few hundred yards through brush and weeds; and it ends with a ranch house that looks like something out of Levittown. Here, on the water, there are real warning signs about private property.

I expect the family gave in to the tragedy and moved to town, and brings a spider plant every June.

The shock of the shrine wears off. Brandon has been given a public mourning, but in an eerie, peculiar way. A walker might see the shrine and wonder. A driver won't even see it. Only the community knows. Grief like this needs no validation from another world, or from me. Yet I wish I knew. But of course I'd be afraid to ask, afraid that I'd be the awkward outsider, hampered as much by temperament as by geography. I would not dare stir up grief (or pry into lives, or presume) in a community like this. I haven't earned it. If a community means natural delight and human responsibility, I've got the first down to my bones, and a very long way to go on the second.

****

On my map, Makers Cove Road is marked Fire Road #43, harking back to the time before Enhanced 9-1-1 forced a more creative naming of Maine roads at the turn of this enlightened century. As if in response to its new status, the northern half of Makers Cove is clearly trying to raise its game. A sign suggests admittance only of owners and their guests, intimating a gated association, with guard dogs. (There is neither, yet.) The road is gravel, but smooth and expertly graded. The driveways leading down to the cove on the west give the illusion of prosperity (nice mailboxes, some plantings, a curve or two to ensure privacy), implying that the houses at their ends would be worthy of glossy magazines if the owners allowed the publicity. Makers Cove is no Bayview Street in Camden, but apparently aspires to be – yet another privatized section of the coast in the making. It's still rural and wooded and quiet down here, but there's a kind of tension in the air, like the repressed glee of a counting room. A garden tour will break out any minute now. I'm sure that any cars parked out of sight have out-of-state plates, and that the houses are closed up in the winter. All this makes that old fishing colony at road's end, mostly decaying, only slightly developing, more endearing.

Just after Makers Cove, the turn to Birch Point appears. I'm on state park property now: suddenly the trees are taller, the woods seem deeper and endless, the gravel road is straight but rutted by budget cuts. A Welcome sign at the end is not very welcoming, mostly full of "don'ts" about booze and pets. In this era of strapped and reviled government, a new collection box asks $2 of Maine residents, $3 of non-residents (on the honor system, of course; Owls Head is too far out-of-the-way to afford a park ranger).

I don't know when the park was founded, when the land was taken or given to protect it. I do know, having been stopped for directions several times on my walks, that locals still know it as Lucia Beach. I also know to distinguish it from the new Lucia Beach just around the eastern point of the park.

You could hardly ask for a greater contrast. Old Lucia, the state park, is a lovely horseshoe of coarse sand strewn with rockweed. Both arms of the embrace are made of pink granite, shelving into the sea. Spruce trees lean seductively over the granite, backed by thousands more. Romantics sit on the ledges, gazing out to sea, a few tanners spread out on beach towels, and their kids poke in tidal pools. The Muscle Ridge Islands offshore emphasize escape. It will be this way forever (we hope).

New Lucia is a tiny pocket beach, whose fine white sand is covered at high tide. Huge boulders don't shelve into the water but stand upright like sentinels. The views out to sea are just as glorious. But the land is cut into a half-dozen lots, each with a house, small, medium, large. There's even a gray, condo-like thing hulking in the middle.

Our political ancestors made refuges. Our present politicians make refugees.

The parking lot at Birch Point Beach State Park is full on warm summer weekends, often overflowing onto the road. Most cars have Maine plates. But how long before CT and MA and NY and NH and MD drive ME away? In my own tentative transition from Massachusetts to Maine, I walk there only on weekday mornings, when it's mostly deserted. Parks were created just for this, to bring the beauty of nature to city dwellers, but when masses of people come, it's as if the city has merely been transplanted. OK, it's not that bad. Don't think the worst, I have to tell myself, don't be a nature snob. Everyone deserves the chance to get out of themselves, out of horsepower or sugar or shopping or Tanqueray or whatever influence under which they try to cope. Unless they bring all this to the beach. Then they are undeserving of nature's purity.

This is the danger of living the way we do, divided, unsettled. Some of us truly love the city, some the country, and some are trying to take the best of both, the last of which may ultimately be impossible. The mobility we now assume, even crave – of jobs, place, house, emotion – hasn't finished fighting with the stability bred from millions of years of evolution. And if Nowhere Man actually wins the battle of DNA? He might already be winning: where Thoreau needed a minimum of four hours a day walking outdoors (he marvels at people who "stay in their shops not only all the forenoon, but all the afternoon too, sitting with crossed legs, so many of them – as if the legs were made to sit upon, and not to stand or walk upon – I think that they deserve some credit for not having all committed suicide long ago"), 150 years later people tell themselves they're content with just a half hour, or a few minutes in a lawn chair, or just a whiff of sea air from a hotel room. We love our boundaries, our safe tethers to Mother Comfort – and we are slowly committing suicide.

The world changes again once I leave the state park and continue on Ballyhac Road. The first time my wife and I came all the way here, we drove. It was lovely, but the drive was over in a couple of minutes and we saw almost nothing. This time, I'm on foot, and all is new: these lovely curves, the road rising and falling like waves in the woods, one white pine fantastically gnarled and twisted like something out of Tolkien, the lobster smack abandoned in the weeds of a small glade, the smell of pines and soon, the tang of the ocean. I didn't realize that on this entire section of the road, at least a mile long, there's only one house, a real Maine house, slightly falling down, yard full of lobster traps and coiled rope and several species of broken-down vehicles. (Of course, where the road ends at the water, there's a large house in excellent suburban condition.) We certainly didn't drive down Dyer Point Road (Fire Road #44) near the end of Ballyhac; the sign "Private" discouraged us.

Other people in cars aren't so discouraged, however, judging by the number of No Parking signs I see as I walk down Dyer Point. Even in our timid culture, the urge to explore the unknown is strong, if the unknown extends only so far as ogling pretty houses on waterfront properties from cars. I understand the urge from two sides, the kind of house porn that lures drivers into the most private of yards, and the fury of those suffering the trespass. I'm guilty of both. But I think it's different for walkers, who provoke fewer territorial reactions than, say, tourists from New Jersey in an Escalade. It's the anonymity of cars that drives shore owners crazy, the entitlement of the trespass, the double glass of windshields and Ray Bans, the protection of sheet metal, the "ignorance" of out-of-state plates, the apparent lack of response when we yell at them, waving our arms, their shrugs as they back into our flowers and rut our driveways and ram our lampposts. What would they have done if we weren't at home? Pressed their oily noses against the windows to view our decor? Set up a picnic on the lawn?

Walkers are less subject to remonstrance. They don't leave ruts and coffee cups behind. It's easier to deal with a hundredweight of flesh than a ton of steel. You can frighten them away with dogs if you're really serious about privacy.

Yet this business of private property remains a sticky one. I feel slightly anxious walking on private roads. I don't know anyone here. There may be dogs. Surely not guns? The same issue arises if I'm walking on the actual shore, for in Maine ocean fronts are owned down to the low-tide mark. How far would someone go to intimidate me? How far would I go to intimidate him back?

But my walk down Dyer Point today is Doberman-less and uneventful, not to mention lovely. There are only half a dozen houses, smallish, gray-shingled, obviously old, no great rooms recently manufactured, no kitchen enlarged because otherwise the new Subzero wouldn't fit. I see no one but a young man mowing; we exchange polite waves and good mornings.

The road seems to end in a driveway and I don't go any farther, even though I guess that the bit of land just off shore must be Spaulding Island and I'd love to know how to get out there. Someone lives there: at the other end of Dyer Point Road, the nest of mailboxes included one that says "1 Spaulding Island." What an address! I would have loved to see a neat parking space at the end of the driveway, and a small dock, maybe a skiff – such signs of another man's heaven would have given me a month's worth of middle-night dreams. Islands are a whole 'nother kind of mania, best saved for an imaginary walk.

Dick, a man I'd meet somewhat later who lives on Dyer Point Road (for almost 50 years now), would have known about "1 Spaulding Island," but I didn't ask at the time, having met him at a business gathering and not caring to be island-envious in public.

The only signs of 21st century stress on Dyer Point Road are a few out-of-state plates, and those No Parking signs. Otherwise it is perfect, a most Thoreau-like marriage of sea and shore and cottage and deep woods at the back, a modest approach to civilization.

But I expect that my reincarnated avatar of Thoreau might not have been entirely happy with walks around Ballyhac. The prescriptions of his great essay "Walking" don't quite exist: not big enough for a whole afternoon of "sauntering," few fields for philosophizing about farmers and shopkeepers, woods not deep enough to qualify as wilderness, a little too much doom of development. The scale is too small; Thoreau always tried to recreate in Concord what he loved in the great forests and mountains of Maine – wilderness and the illusion of it. He didn't really want to deal with the idea of private property, even though, or especially because, he made his living as a surveyor. In "Walking" he blithely saunters through woods and fields and across all manner of property lines, and rather throws away the following line: "To enjoy a thing exclusively is commonly to exclude yourself from the true enjoyment of it." I'd like to think that the development battles of the 21st century would force him to think more deeply about the idea of private property. Although what is a motto for the land trust movement is the line that immediately follows: "Let us improve our opportunities, then, before the evil days come."

I think about this on a later day as I walk a path that Dick told me about. The start of the path isn't very obvious from the Dyer Point side, he said, especially in summer when it's quite overgrown, but it traverses Otter Point all the way to the trails of the state park and is a lovely walk. He was right.

I have started from the state park side, not trusting my orienteering instincts. Here the path is pretty obvious for a while. Lots of feet have trod here, seeking a bit of Maine wildness past the beach boys and the beach blankets. Gradually, however, the path grows fainter and I realize I must have left the park and am now walking on private land. Unlike the more developed parts of the state, there is no sign warning me of trespass, and the path continues invitingly just above the shore, just above the granite ledge that slides into the sea, through the pine stands, over mossy rocks, over fallen trees. A path along the ocean in Maine is like no other. Pine needles pack the route, underbrush has been stripped away by the winds, and weak trees succumb to the same, leaving only the big and strong and spaces between them. Views of the water are nearly continuous. At any number of places you can easily leave the path and sit on the ledge for a moment or an hour of poetry.

Soon the path becomes a little harder to follow. Nobody from the park cares to come this far, judging by the number of spider webs I break. I have to backtrack a couple of times from false paths, climbing over tree trunks splintered by storms, walking through patches of bunchberries, their red fruit and low, shiny leaves glowing like holiday holly. I find the path again just before it passes a boarded-up, one-room cottage on the shore. Someone owns all of Otter Point, and perhaps uses this cottage on occasion, but in good 19th-century fashion allows those in the know to walk in timelessness.

Isn't this what we all crave? Insider knowledge? A sense of belonging to a place? A community of people who would mourn you, would erect a shrine to you? Like Thoreau, I don't want an exclusive contract of use but one to share with other, like-minded souls, those who tread lightly and reverently. Unlike Thoreau, I have to think about the pressures of population, about people who break down doors, pitch beer cans into the ocean, and race dirt bikes in the woods. This is the dilemma of the conservation movement: I'm telling you about the glories of this path, but if it were to become popular and remained unsupervised, it would inevitably change for the worse. The owner of Otter Point allows access to this land, but that one-room cottage's windows are thickly boarded, and the metal door is dented badly as if besieged, and two padlocks secure it against the public. I'm not necessarily saying people are naturally destructive. I'm saying it takes only a few cigarette butts and Doritos bags to start a chain of abuse, a psychology of neglect and carelessness, and the sheer pressure of population and development makes that abuse inevitable.

Thoreau's avatar might even have come around to believe in private land management – or at least the best of it, by trusts, government, and wealthy individuals – because it enforces responsible and judicious use. He who hated bureaucracy would have no choice but to applaud the committees, the guilt money, the volunteer land stewards, and even the endless paperwork. At all cost, we need our natural places to walk.

Past the one-room cottage, the path becomes overgrown. My city self worries about poison ivy and ticks; my country self pushes through the weeds, bare legs and all. The quiet is all-encompassing. The airport seems far away. After a few minutes I see a lobster boat anchored offshore, and a house or two comes into view across the cove, and the path ends in a lawn belonging to that big house at the end of Ballyhac Road. I don't care to trespass, or provoke. I'm a big tall stranger. I won't put someone in a position of ire, or fear.

There's another route out to the road, I'm sure, and I backtrack, now into deeper woods and on a trail even fainter. Away from the shore, I lose my bearings slightly. That queasy feeling of anxiety arises, the one about intimidators (but not wild ones – they don't bear malice). I think I see the trail, but woods can be featureless and direction is easily lost. We seldom allow ourselves to be lost. It's a nice scary feeling.

OK, I tell myself, you are hardly in deep wilderness, you are no Thoreau climbing Katahdin without compass or companion. There's little danger in Owls Head. You'll run into something familiar eventually.

And then I see white blazes on trees, helpfully painted for the rurally impaired, and I follow them and soon enough come out into a small field. The ground is slightly boggy and the field's been recently mowed, whether for hay or for esthetics, I don't know. I'm both disappointed and relieved to see this trace of human industry. I might have liked to be lost for a while longer.

I cross the field to Ballyhac Road and see the mailboxes for Dyer Point and think of going up to Dick's house and thanking him for the entrée to this Sainte Terre. But I don't, for the illusion of self-reliance is too pleasant, and I walk back up Ballyhac, towards Dublin Road and the roar of the airport.

Airport

In 1939 the City of Rockland built an airport in the Town of Owls Head. From what I know, or care to find out, of its subsequent development I can construct only a bare-bones skeleton. There were politics, I expect, and the profit motive, and payoffs, and undoubtedly a bit of US War Department engineering behind the scenes, considering that Maine was the closest state to the threat of German Nazism. Imagine the patronage as the airport, endangering and polluting the town that never owned it, changes hands through the decades: Rockland and the feds establish it; in 1941 the Navy drops the pretense and takes over, but cedes it to the City again when war funds dry up: during Maine's bad years in the 50s and 60s, Rockland seeks help and money from Knox County, which finally takes over in 1968; the County runs out of money and petitions the federal government for funding, which (surprise) worked then and forever since. Even today Knox County Regional Airport dominates poor little Owls Head, consuming about a tenth of its acreage and most of its attention. Its two runways cross like chopsticks discarded at the end of a meal. Its two airlines make money only because they're subsidized by the feds for "essential services," mainly to the islands of Penobscot Bay. This is an old story in America, this expanding definition of "essential."

Around the airport's edges lie a few patches of preserved wetland, a bone tossed to conservationists during the expansion in the 1990s. Before 1939, the whole area had been wetlands, and traditional Mainers might have said good riddance, just useless swamps anyway. Owls Head back then would have been full of such folks, farmers and fishermen and foresters mostly, whose proud devotion to land and sea was compellingly complemented by their suspicion of the feds, not to mention suspicion of another kind of swampland, Franklin Roosevelt's New Deal and the "We Poke Alongs" of the WPA. But I imagine the lure of all that federal money, the novelty of air travel, and the un-productivity of marshes greased everyone's palms, if not consciences. Subsequently, as is probably true for every airport in the world, central government propped up Knox County Regional and funded all improvements, including the most recent construction of a new terminal in 2011. As far as I can tell, citizens at the annual town meetings never turned down any of the money, hardly discussed it at all, in fact.

But enough of facts. What I really care about has little to do with politics or patronage. When I walk around the airport, brave its terminal, even trespass on its runway, when under its flight path over my house I read novels or split wood or just gaze at the sea, I care as much about its symbolism as its reality. Imagination puts flesh on the crossbones of that runway skeleton, imagination populates dreams and nightmares. I imagine that every Gulfstream's a dragon to slay, or at least I flip it the finger when it roars overhead.

Planes are the symbol of human dominance, and perhaps our demise. Motors rule us even as they seem to provide escape from rule. And in August, the month we crave all year, Maine's signature season, they are loudest and fullest: cars and boors in traffic jams, mowers and blowers and saws on the land, power-, lobster-, jetski-, and cigarette-boats on the water, and an incessant stream of planes taking off into the prevailing southerly winds.

****

The airport was created out of some 500 acres of swamp. I don't imagine that any wetlands commissions protested. I don't imagine there were any conservation groups at all back then in this neglected, ordinary part of the world. But not all of the swamp is gone; in 1995, when the airport proposed to lengthen its runways and install an Instrument Landing System (and the year my wife and I bought a house in Owls Head in ignorance of the onslaught of personal jets newly enabled), a few activists extracted some "mitigation" from the County.

Not that you'd notice the wetlands if you drive by. They are just a few damp spots here and there on the perimeter of the fences, tucked into the armpits of the crossed runways. In walking by, however, you get a faint echo of the past, very faint, I have to say, because all you can see are reeds and grasses, and you'd like to assume there are a few turtles, waterfowl, or muskrats hidden away; but all you can hear until the next plane lands is wind rustling and one bird singing; all you can smell is a little exhaust. That rich, moist bog-smell is too far away, hidden behind a chain-link security fence. The best you can do is focus your eyes through and beyond the fence, to make it disappear; for a moment or two of imagination the wetlands yield up their past glories, perhaps in a vision of thousands of wood ducks, or a rookery of great blue herons.

Well, something is better than nothing, goes the old apology, the County is going to upgrade the place anyway, anything wild at all improves on this giant field mowed like a suburban lawn and scattered with rich people's playthings. You can't walk around unfocused and cross-eyed and dreamy all the day. You have to face the facts.

But there's no denying that the big, new, noisy, silver birds got the best of the deal; the small quiet brown ones got some cattails on a couple of acres. The noise of motors, sporadic though it may be at a small facility, is such that I'm embarrassed on behalf of what wildlife remains.

On this Monday morning, late-ish, I've walked the mile up Ash Point Drive to the airport, and am now stepping foot on its property for the first time in 16 years of living here. (We drove in once, a ride of two hundred yards on Airport Road, just for the hell of it. We didn't get out of the car.) In the new terminal the rush from a busy August weekend is over. Four people are visible: a TSA guard behind a desk, a man standing at the windows looking out on the runways, an older woman dusting curios in the Blue Yonder, the new airport shop, and a younger woman with a shoulder bag and backpack half-lying in a molded plastic seat, perhaps sleeping. They seem to rattle around in space (almost 10,000 square feet of it, I discover later), as if they are emissaries from the future for the crowds that will inevitably come. If the feds are paying, why not spend the $3 million or $4 million and build far beyond your current needs, especially when your former arrivals hall was a double-wide trailer so embarrassing for the jet set? I nod to the TSA guy and leave. Perhaps the golden future will not arrive for a while.

Outside, the trailer is still there, re-purposed for car rentals. Across one runway sit the hangers and puddle-jumpers of the Knox County Flying Club, and across the other runway stands the Owls Head Transportation Museum. There's only one jet on the tarmac, of the small but luxurious kind that the wealthy use "to get away to the Maine house" for a few days.

On my 1978 map of Owls Head this place is merely called Municipal Airport, somehow a more friendly and hopeful designation. It's not very friendly anymore. Shortly after the new ILS went in, the town was forced to put up a small sign on adjacent Dublin Road advertising a noise-complaint phone number to call. Simple Cessnas are one thing, but ILS had brought in the jets. I and other neighbors directly under one of the flight paths have called many times, comically shouting at a recording about late-night and early-morning violations of the "suggested" guidelines for airport use. No one has ever called us back, or reported at town meeting on the number of calls recorded and certainly not on the decibel level of anger. The necessities of businessmen and the glamour of movie stars with mansions on nearby islands trump our petty concerns. "Grow up," the selectmen would say. "That's life." And it is – I myself have exploited airplanes and airports hundreds of times in service to my career.

Perhaps the complaints did produce a response. Eventually Knox County published a booklet on noise for the instruction of pilots using the airport. Called "Noise Abatement" on its website, the thing actually discusses Noise Compatibility. A subtle distinction? I quote as the booklet talks to pilots:

"Owls Head is a quiet fishing community on the pristine coast of Maine. Knox County employs a noise complaint hotline which residents may call in the event of excessive aircraft noise. Please observe the recommended Noise Compatibility Program. Like all communities having an airport in their midst, our airport neighbors understand the need for the airport, but are appreciative of any efforts to reduce aircraft noise and low flying. We offer the following voluntary procedures for arrival and departure and count on responsible pilots to follow them."

Clearly, private enterprise rules this airport, in spite of the anomalous "pristine." Very little is actually prohibited, including violating curfew hours, and flying too low over the Noise Sensitive Area in which our house sits. And don't you love it when the government speaks for us, we the understanding "airport neighbors"?

I obsess about airplanes because every sight of a jet, every sound from any kind of airplane, every flight over our house provokes a revisitation of a former life. The past echoes: I hear the roar of a take-off, and jumbled images follow and plague me, of sales presentations, client meets, rooms at the Hyatt, over-drinking and -eating, of ambition and stress and jetlag – all the anxious hallmarks of international business. I'm convinced there's a direct line from Boeing engines to gastric reflux.

Yet the public continues to fly, more than ever. Tiny Knox County records steady passenger increases. Planes get bigger: Airbus builds a plane that could seat more than half of Owls Head's population. Every airport in the world seems to be under construction. The County will soon build a bigger fence – for $1.3 million – to keep out deer and turkeys. Each landing brings money, ideas, ambition, disease. Business travelers are bagmen for the multinational mafia, with a little self-interest thrown in.

In effect, all this activity means more development of the land. I worked in publishing, a so-called clean industry; let's say I travel to Paris to persuade the International Society on Hemostasis and Thrombosis to start a new scientific journal. Besides the obvious carbon cost of travel, it sounds innocuous, right? But that journal's individual success will consume trees, watts, more meetings and more travel, and in the aggregate, the sale of journals and cars and cornflakes makes companies grow, which means new offices and parking lots and longer runways with ILS even in rural Maine. This is how the world works: personal ambition sucking up to international capitalism.

The car shrank America until the continent got full. Now the plane shrinks the planet so that every other country on it can also get full.

I look back at the terminal building, imagining roles for the FAA and the TSA in some new enlightened world. Businesses will be ranked according to their environmental insults; the worst get the fewest flying credits. Business travelers will be so branded in a database. TSA will scan their retinas and record compliance.

Fine for me to say – I already got mine. I travelled without restriction in the service of profit. I made my nut. I survived, or did I? What damage does this restlessness do? What price did I really pay (the price of complicity if nothing else)? And the carbon crisis grows apace, and each contrail is an omen in the sky, and each mail plane from Matinicus buzzing over my deck, each Gulfstream connecting with New York, carries a manifest of ruin.

In the course of 25 years of business travel I remember a thousand anxious take-offs from Boston's Logan – but then, in recompense, a thousand lovely approaches, over Boston's bucolic western suburbs, or over the islands of Boston Harbor glistening in the setting sun, coming back home to my family. Thank God, I murmur, I've weathered another trip. Tension drains. Our vacation in Maine is now a little closer, I'm a little closer to driving out of the city and onto Route 1 and walking into the house and seeing Penobscot Bay and feeling my stomach lining give thanks. I suppose I should thank the mafia for all this, now that I take the cure much more frequently. I suppose I shouldn't curse every time yet another plane shakes the window glass. Maybe someone on that Learjet is coming home.

It's clear why the government spends so much on transportation. It encourages restlessness and movement and activity, i.e., increases taxes. Travel is like a drug: an opiate for your present pain, a stimulant for your future fancies.

Now in a slight daze myself, I leave the terminal area and wander down Brenner Lane, a road that runs along the airport fence for a quarter mile or so. It ends in an inviting path: green, sheltered by trees, almost wide enough for a vehicle. I don't know where it goes but no invitation is necessary. I'm out walking my town. But soon I realize that the airport fence has disappeared, and then the path ends too, rather abruptly, and spills me out of the woods into hot, open air. For a minute I'm disoriented, but then I realize I'm about to walk on a runway and I hold back, imagining the headlines in the Herald Gazette: "Massachusetts Man Seized on Airport's Runway - No Terrorist Link Yet Found."

OK, so it's not an active runway, it's the third one, now disused, built in the war years when the airport was called Ash Point Naval Air Station, but still....if I were fanatically persuaded, I could just....It would be so easy....Well, I'll never get a chance to do this at Logan so why not take it?

I leave the protection of trees, venture into the open. At the far end of the runway I can see the low, sprawling, corrugated buildings of the Owls Head Transportation Museum (another place I've not yet set foot in, a penance for another day). At the near end, there's a small hangar, just a few hundred yards of cracked concrete away, maybe there's a way out to Ash Point Drive from there. I could always backtrack to the terminal, what a person from away would do. But a completed circle on these walks feels more like an accomplishment than craven back-tracking, and if I'm accosted, I can always plead ignorance, just out for a walk, sir, checking in the terminal on flights to Boston, and I saw this nice path....

Quickly, I walk toward the hangar, looking for a way out. The airport fence and a big locked gate appear on one side of the hangar, looking terribly official, but on the other side, there is no barrier at all. So much for security. My innocence and ignorance are rewarded, and in the country way, as if I were a local, I sidle around the building and emerge on Ash Point Drive, safe from the clutches of TSA.

I still marvel a bit at walking on an airport runway. It's as if Owls Head is living in a different time. It's as if the airport never got the memo about the 9/11 terrorists and their overnight in Maine. It's as if the relationship between a government and a citizenry could be benign after all.

I won't ever be friends with the airport. But dreamy, mushy, entitled thinking, say, on a deck, on a perfect morning on the coast of Maine, with birds and surf, should be periodically punctured, right? It brings this spaceman down to earth.

****

The post-World War II years were not prosperous in Maine. While the rest of the country was booming, Maine struggled with its traditional, resource-bound economy. Fishing, farming, forestry, textiles, and ship-building were being overtaken by big competitors out west and overseas and little was taking their place. Tourism was still just a blip on the financial charts. There were no such things as locavores, or software, or "the creative industries." By 1968 the City of Rockland was no longer able to maintain the airport profitably and turned over its management to Knox County.

Airport

It's completely coincidental that 1968 also saw Ed Muskie, Maine's Democratic Senator, nominated as Hubert Humphrey's running mate. It's also coincidental, but deeply symbolic, that Muskie's career – re-invigorator of Maine's Democratic Party, Maine's Governor in the late 50s, US Senator for more than 20 years, Secretary of State under Jimmy Carter, one of the first conservationists and a strong proponent of the great federal environmental legislation of the 60s and 70s – came to end with the election of Ronald Reagan in 1980, from whose politics of greed the nation may never recover.

The flower children abandoned the land. Corporations have gained the rights of citizens. Development is more important than nature. That's how I see it, at least, that's how I interpret the present, this new and terrible chapter in America's history, so redolent of the rapacious 19th century, and when I leave the airport and walk back home along Ash Point Drive, I see Ilvonen Lane branching off into the woods and remember that, a few years ago, my wife and I had seen a kind of subdivision promised back there, before the real estate meltdown. We thought, "Now what are 'they' doing, those bad guys." Coastal property had been at such a premium before 2008 that even near-coastal property was developing quickly, even lots here in the middle of nowhere, without waterfront, under the airport's flight path. Apparently not even rural Maine could escape land grabs.

The development we saw then was called Ledgewood Estates: a few numbered lots, half-cleared land, half-paved roads, some very lonely utility poles. What I see today, post-recession, has hardly changed. A big map still advertises 12 life-changing lots. Three of them are now marked "Sold," which I hardly believe, for when I walk in there's no development whatsoever, still the same lot numbers on stakes mostly hidden by weeds, the lots still featuring stumps and mounds of dirt, birch trees standing around in tears, a bit of road newly surfaced but obviously nobody drives here, for weeds are growing directly out of the tar. There's a terrible forlornness here, a gash in the woods. And "Ledgewood" still makes no sense: where's the ledge? What kind of wood grows on rock? Was this someone's dream project, or just a ploy to make a quick buck? Did those three lots sell to people with visions of suburbia in the woods, or were they just speculators as well?

Let's assume the positive. Let's assume that 12 lucky families would plan to enjoy the best that America has to offer, a subdivision surrounded by woods, suburban gardens watched over by deer, cable available, houses circled to keep out the bad guys, and fewer than 5 miles away the big-box stores and theaters and gas stations of civilization. Most of us would jump at the chance, wouldn't we? Most of us grew up in the real suburbs, miles and miles of them, next to a real city, far away from wildlife, in the middle of the stress of making a middle-class living. How wonderful to escape all that! And in Maine besides!

But of course this is a fiction. For one thing, capitalism failed this little subdivision, unable to sustain yet another bubble. Only the well-off bought property in the recession, and Knox County does not have a lot of well-off people. And then only a tiny percentage of pioneers would actually leave the city and its suburbs in the first place.

But there are many people, like us, who want both city and country. They are an ambitious breed, these rural wannabes, your basic stay-at-homes often forced to travel to press flesh or win money, thinking of escaping from the "Good Life" to the good life. They think of Maine, for example, knowing instinctively that life in the city is hard and demands a release, a dream world, a chance to fulfill life-long desires imperfectly squelched by the getting of capital. Then they get serious and buy property, and each time they arrive and catch sight of the water, tension starts to drain, responsibilities flake off, and that feeling of reaching one's real potential, if just given the time, is reawakened.

For most of that first week of August vacation, positives battle negatives. The deck is sat upon, the bay is gazed at, our refugees play games with the children, they pick raspberries and make pies, they dabble with their writing, or painting, or photography, but for several days the birds are mere shapes in the sky, and the gardens a matter of weeds, not glories, and they can't seem to shake the habit of watching TV after dinner or listening to the news.

By week two, Maine has got them organized. They live to the rhythm of the tides more than the flux of the stomach acid. The gardens are diagrammed again. The birds – loons, ducks, ospreys, finches – regain their etymologies. The words come a little easier to paper. The whole family sits on the deck after dinner, watching the ospreys dive in the cove, until dark. But all too soon it's time to return home. They walk with the kids to the pink granite ledges one last time to touch starfish and gaze at the foggy sea with a fierce longing, as if to fix it in the mind like a shroud.

The Maine glow lasts until about noon of their first day back at work, in the reality of awaiting importunities – in the eighties the stack of pink "While You Were Out" telephone messages and the piled-up In-Box; the queue of voicemails in the nineties; the aughts' email onslaught. Maine reverts to a dream, the thing that cuts through the stress and the worry like a canoe through water, the hope that lingers throughout the year, in board meetings and airports, under the scope of the gastroenterologist and the beam of the therapist. The memory of those few weeks in the summer, those holiday weekends throughout the year makes bearable the daily commute through the heart of rush-hour Boston, a dreamy, temporary commutation of one's sentence to hard labor to pay for the dream in the first place.

And even for them, is it a fiction? Maine may be a fantasy as long as they don't live there – the anti-suburbs, the dream to get out of the American dream. And the season of revisitation, how long will that last before they must choose between sidewalk and seashore?

****

On the other end of the third, disused runway is that museum for motors, the Owls Head Transportation Museum, enshrining both dominant varieties: the automobile, which contributed most to America's change; and the airplane, which may be an even better symbol of the military-industry-government complex. It's now my turn to pay a little homage and for the first time ever (that's 16 years' worth of ever, and about to start the count over because I don't ever expect to again) I set foot inside the OHTM.

I've driven today, for it's a little too far to walk all the way around the airport for potentially so little gain, but I have not driven quite all the way. I've parked at the end of Museum Road, where it meets Route 73. There's a cleared space for several cars there, and one car already parked, and I briefly wonder why. The Museum is at least a half-mile away.

Museum Road itself is lovely, wide as a city boulevard, quiet and curved as a country lane with no end in sight, and surrounded by large trees that haven't been harvested for a while. It's a quiet Tuesday morning and only a couple of cars make their way to and from the museum. As I walk, I see a path into the woods to the left and make a mental note to explore it on the way back.

Mind you, when I get to the Museum, I don't tour it. That would imply an homage, and ten bucks, too far. I just look in on the lobby, worry briefly about the moose (is it stuffed?) standing just inside the door, and quickly walk back outside, slightly embarrassed. Cars aren't quite my thing, although I did own a hotdog Mercury Capri once…. Behind the museum the antique-car-auction action is starting to build for the weekend. Guys in T-shirts look at muscle cars. Couples of a certain age walk around Cadillacs from the Fabulous Fifties as if remembering their fathers. There are Model Ts and a Fokker Red Baron and a surfeit of Corvettes and a couple of tourists waiting for the 20-minute Coastal Biplane Ride. It's starting to get hot, sun glaring on metal, softening tar. I feel quite out of place, needing a baseball cap at least, or a tree.

On the way back to the car, I take that path and it turns out to be surprising, offering at least a couple of miles of hiking. I walk through birch forests and boggy places and one perfect glade full of ferns and long grasses, where I stop for a moment. An open place like this is arresting, but I'm not sure why. Contrast with deep woods, of course – humans demand the constant stimulation of change, that sudden change in scale, to plants and spaces smaller than us, controllable. I have the suspicion that it was cleared by lightning, or by people for a cabin, whereupon my reveries go voyeuristic, imagining motives of escape, someone's peaceful nights, and then abandonment from boredom or fire or old age. But why haven't the trees reclaimed it? Lacy ferns even in profusion seem too weak to withstand the onslaught of conifer cones. Perhaps humans have permanently contaminated these soils, leaving them to the lovers of light and damp.

Throughout this walk there's that familiar, anxious, but completely engrossing feeling of not knowing where I'm going, not knowing who might challenge me for my trespasses, not knowing where I'll end up. To have enough time to explore in woods: how wonderful, not to mention the contrast with Corvettes. No schedule – just the need for lunch, eventually. And eventually I find the end of the path, of course; I've looped around, back to Museum Road. And there's the sign I missed when I first parked the car. Paul D. Merriam Nature Park, it says, apparently an adjunct to the OHTM. Ah, I say to myself, somewhat ashamed now at having smiled fatuously at the same sign next to the museum, where there seemed only to be a picnic table, a climbing structure and a quarter acre of trees. I see now there's a lot more to this park than a lunch spot for tourists. It conserves a couple of hundred acres of quiet, undeveloped woods (and the trails total four miles on both sides of the entrance road, as I discover later).

Ah, and it's a strange world when a large block of woods sits right next to two such temples to development, when a museum dedicated to man's motors boasts no better symbol of wildness than a moose, when these walking trails that owe their origin and allegiance to machines carry a sign banning use of ATVs and snowmobiles, when a Nature Park honoring a lost way of life is missed, or ignored, by thousands of old-car nuts whizzing by, when one doesn't know what exists in one's own backyard.

I talk to myself as I walk along busy Route 73 (the only numbered state road in Owls Head, by the way, and less than two miles' worth), completing my foot-mileage in this part of town. Is this the future of the environmental movement, development mitigated by the setting aside of a few acres here and there, resulting in sterile islands bounded by asphalt? The woods of the nature center are lovely, and on the other side of 73 there's a sweeping view of cleared fields and a marsh in the distance, a compelling reason for another visit, but the woods seemed curiously devoid of bird or any other life, and now the traffic thunders by, and houses and businesses appear, and I reach familiar Ash Point Drive a mile later.

To redeem the anxiety of this walk I need at least to complete the circle back to the car. There must be a path back through the woods to the nature center, and I walk slowly down Smalls Lane, a little road that parallels Ash Point. One place looks promising but soon fades into a field of sumac. I fail to find anything else like a trail. I'm sure locals know one. I'm not local. I have to backtrack on Route 73, walking twice where no one ever walks.

That even such a scattered approach to land preservation has to rely on the private sector, such as land trusts and wealthy Rockefellers funding museums, is a little shameful. No level of government – local, county, state, federal – seems to believe in good deeds anymore. We spend our capital on stimulus. We try to buy our way out of trouble. Our answer to climate change is to create an economy of carbon credits.

And what about public works? Build more roads is the answer, use more tar. Any hope of a new WPA for the good of people is a pipe dream. Everything must have a monetary benefit. Can you imagine the hoots in Congress today if someone proposed a new Federal Writers' Project (alumni in the 30s: Saul Bellow, John Cheever, Richard Wright, John Steinbeck, Ralph Ellison)?

Back home I follow up on my discoveries and get cheered up again. That marsh off Route 73, according to the Shoreland Zoning Map on the town's website, is indeed another protected area I didn't know about. In fact it's called a "Resource Protection for Moderate and High Value Freshwater Wetlands as rated by Inland Fish and Wildlife." I wonder if it's available for public use – the prospect of another new walk is exhilarating. Another one beckons: the map shows a little corner of Resource Protection land where Owls Head and South Thomaston meet at the Weskeag River and marsh. And then I look up the Nature Park and find Paul D. Merriam.

His obituary is inspiring: a 94-year-long life full of work and family and people and volunteering and hiking. He was prominent in almost innumerable organizations, like his church, local schools, the Masons, historical societies, Kiwanis, Audubon Society, environmental groups. He was assistant postmaster for Rockland. His children include a poet and a historian. His great-grandchildren number 19; there's even a great-great-granddaughter. His family clearly adored him. He seemed to have been able to mix development and preservation. He seemed to be a simple man, able to deal with the contradictions of loving motors, loving trees.

Like any place on earth, Owls Head is full of contradictions, but here the problem is that it's too easy to sit on the shore or walk in the woods and ignore the daily dilemmas in the cities, or just down the street. That's why all these loud motors – planes, cars, chainsaws, mowers – may actually be beneficial. That jet hissing and snarling overhead is like the snake in paradise, a humbling reminder of real life on present earth.

Heavenly reprieves are, well, heavenly, but it doesn't do for old Calvinists like me, however lapsed, to expect the world of them.

Ingraham's Hill

The highest point in Owls Head is Ingraham's Hill, which, at only 200 feet above sea level, isn't saying much. But it gains most of that elevation somewhat abruptly, between the ocean shore and Route 73, making it a headland and a beacon. I assume Native Americans used it so, for millennia, as they fished the waters of Penobscot Bay. I know the Europeans did, starting with that day in 1605 that brought the adventurer Champlain, the first of the culprits, to Owls Head. He didn't stay around to exploit anybody or anything, but inevitably, hearing of wood and fur and cod, then limestone in the hills, then granite in the islands, then postcard views for their vacation homes, others did.

By the 18th century, immigrants from Europe were building houses and burying bodies in what amounted to a small town, with church and school and store, and for the next 300 years, and especially after the Industrial Revolution, the slopes of the hill added encroachments – what might be called suburbs if so small a town as Owls Head can have a suburb – from the city of Rockland to the north. The latter half of the 20th century contributed three wide, asphalt roads that climb up the rest of the hill, away from the shore and Route 73 and the lower classes, and gash the woods with houses.

Ingraham's Hill is now the densest part of town, complete with subdivisions. Most of the open spaces and lanes that remain from the old times have been filled in.

I've taken a September morning to walk south from the Rockland line down Route 73 (quaintly called Ingraham Lane by the post office and Google Maps) for a mile, first to explore all of the short, eastward "Lanes" going down to the ocean, and then, coming back north, to attempt the longer, more modern "Drives" taking the gradual incline to the west.

The north side of the hill, that obvious extension of Rockland, seems to be more seasonal, less neighborly, denser, one street ending in a B&B, for example, and another sporting a line of rental cottages packed so closely together as if to mimic the Jersey shore. The road names are literalist, a throwback to prosaic times: Harborside, Ocean, Cottage. But when I get to the top of the hill, the start of the old Ingraham's, I can no longer call what I see the suburbs. The suburbs I've known have been planned, homogenous. This place is not; these neighborhoods are cut haphazardly by lanes that twist down to the sea and remind me more of small Minnesota towns I've lived in and visited (minus the sea, of course, and hills altogether): a range of houses from ranches and Cape Cods to saltboxes and converted sheds, and even a trailer or two; a variety of lot sizes; most gardens and lawns obsessed over, religiously neat and over-trimmed and gnomed to death, some defiantly not, messy and uncut; few people doing anything outside but getting into cars; and those cars all American vehicles with Maine plates. Down by the shore, there are no mansions and no "Massholes," in spite of the million-dollar views of Rockland harbor and the Fox Islands and Owls Head Light. These parts were settled when waterfront property was prized more for commerce than for viewscape.

It also reminds me of the poor towns of Washington County way Down East, far from the pressures of post-war population growth, with their small, weather-beaten houses and modest shore frontage – poor in worldly goods, that is. There's nothing fancy in this part of Owls Head either, not even on the shores of what the realtors call "bold" Penobscot Bay. But in these modest dwellings might live riches of tradition, if not outright belief in a slower way of life.

The names of the lanes here are evocative and personal, memorializing English settlers called Everett, Guptil and Knowlton. One imagines tough fishermen, tenacious farmers, mercenaries, revolutionaries. Head of Bay Cemetery, bordering the road at a high point, as if the grave of a sailor deserves a view of the sea, is full of these former Brits; the grave of one Samuel

Bartlett, 1748-1813, is the earliest one I find. These first American settlers of Ingraham's Hill may have been restless like the rest of us, wandering from their homes for food or work or lust, but they didn't re-locate for "happiness," or career enhancement, I wager, and they came back to their family places to die in peace.

Reluctantly, I leave the cemetery, and the hill, and the 18th century, and walk down 73 to the south, whereupon the houses become much newer, only a few decades old. I know this from the Owls Head Fire Department map, on which the cartographer inked in not only the roads but all houses of the time as well, and on which many of today's houses (and a number of roads) do not appear. The changes in 35 years are what you'd expect, a little more of everything. But down here, on the new side of the hill, the names have become more pretentious, more nostalgic – Clamshell and Head of Bay and even exotic Peaquot (sic) – as if the new generation was trying to connect to a more vivid past. I sympathize with the sentiment. My own sense of nostalgia is strong but stops, I'm afraid, at the Industrial Revolution, where it loses any romance.

Those of us who grew up in suburbia are well familiar with this exodus of moving from the personal to the anodyne, from headland to flatland, from inner suburbs just younger than their parent cities to distant exurbs. Our civilization progresses and spreads, not on the backs of horses or the decks of lobster smacks, but in the terrible comfort of power windows and superhighways, and we lose touch not only with ancestor and neighbor, but with soil and rockweed, red-winged blackbird and loon besides. On the old part of Ingraham's Hill, at least I see a few names on mailboxes that I also see in the cemetery, and in spite of the obvious difficulty of life, which is visible in the flaking paint and the old trucks, in the plastic on the windows; in spite of the modesty of abodes, and lack of power boats and fancy docks; or perhaps because of all this, I suspect that rootedness and tradition in a place like this count for much more than urban and suburban America may remember, or ever know again.

Self-sufficiency, however modest, has its price. Hypocrisy and gossip, xenophobia and small-mindedness surely exist in this place just as they did in the flatlands of my youth. But in Maine, as in most of New England, I've found that life is more often leavened with tolerance than burdened by spite. Maybe the ghosts of all those ancestors keep folks in check. Your great-great grandfather lying in Head of Bay Cemetery might not look kindly on you if you lost your friends to malice, or your soul to money.

I reach the intersection of North Shore Drive and turn around to walk back north on 73. As I came south, I could hardly ignore those three wide roads going west, obviously leading into classic suburban developments. At least they weren't named by stringing nature nouns together, "Pheasant Hollow Run," for example, or something to do with vistas. The developers stuck to the facts more or less, and the three drives, south to north, from the 50s to the 70s to the 90s, are called Bayside West and Harbour Hill (but do note the "u") and Freedom, respectively. Still, the etymologies here strike me as significant, these drives versus the lanes across the way, the former implying vehicles and the latter implying hedges, and what does that tell us about the way America has developed?

I think about just continuing on 73, ignoring these places of tract housing and instant landscaping. They will bring out the worst in me, I know, prejudices and resentments and judgments. Until settling down as an adult, I lived in small towns and new developments and inner cities and outer cities, constantly on the move thanks to a father's callings, and all the while craving permanence. I'm on the edge of finding it in Maine, but these drives are reminders of my uncertainties, and our peculiar unsettled American way of life. It's a struggle some days to appreciate the work of humans, our pollution of land and air and water, our destruction of species including, some day, our own.

Some days I rant and hector. And it's a very warm day, excellent for complaining, and I've already spent two hours meandering along the shore and through more interesting pasts, and damn, it's hot, it shouldn't be this hot on a September morning in Maine.

My mission, however, perhaps a silly one, requires me to walk the length of every road in Owls Head, and I gird up the loins of the mind, prepared for battle.

As I walk into the first development, I wonder if it helps or hurts to imagine Ingraham's Hill as it used to be. It would have been completely forested, of course, for millennia. As the Europeans settled in, it was cleared for farming like the rest of New England, but when the riches of the West lured away the restless and the adventurous and the poor, the forest gradually returned. And now, in the space of 50 years, America having won most of its several wars and prospered, the west side of Ingraham's Hill has become a stark emblem of the new mix of city and country: three long streets regularly laid out and worthy of any urban outskirts; one little reclaimed farm; one large remaining piece of woods.

Okay, I see that the houses on Bayside West are not exactly tract housing. They're nice houses, in fact, mostly Colonials in great variety and set on two- and three-acre lots, much nicer than anything I lived in as a child. Here we have uniform neatness and care. Each house is set chastely back from the road, with lawns and flower gardens; the drive will end, I predict, in a classic cul-de-sac. Some trees have been retained to border the road. Yards seem to back onto woods.

But the development has not been finished. There are many lots un-built (and a look at the town's property tax maps confirms it). In fact, none of these three developments reached its goals. All of them have vacancies. And yet they kept on coming, these wounds in the country. Three separate developments within a half-mile, three separate generations – Bayside West hosting the post-war promise, Harbour Hill the

Great Society dream, Freedom Drive the post-Reagan exuberance, each one building bigger houses on bigger lots. The drive for the American dream seems especially wasteful here.

I'd like to think that the original owners of the land, perhaps farmers, or descendants of sea captains, or just nature lovers, held their properties for a long time, and then fell sick, or got old, and the kids didn't want the land or wanted the money more, and therefore they succumbed easily to developers making pitches. For who can resist a vision of a warm and secure retirement in Florida, especially when beautifully rendered prospectuses of big houses on your land persuade you of the gratefulness of the people who would build them and live there happily ever after?

But apparently a bit of farming still lives on here. I stop walking on Bayside (it seems endless) and a little farther up Route 73 I find Headacre Farm Road. There are a few small houses at its beginning and then I stop and go no farther. I've walked into what is obviously a farmyard.

To someone raised in cities, a farm is somewhat intimidating: fences (what dangers are trying to get out?), vicious-looking vehicles, mud in the yard and things worse, bad smells, gruff men in overalls, dogs never tied up. I should be able to deal with it; I spent several weeks in successive childhood summers on a farm, my grandparents' in Minnesota, that boasted all such attributes. But yet I'm nervous. Respectfully, I leave, even though I'm pretty sure that a farmer is much more likely than, say, a suburbanite, to welcome further exploration of his world.

Or in this case, hers: a subsequent Google search tells me Headacre Farm is operated by a woman on behalf of its owner, a chef, for whom she grows fruits and vegetables to serve at his Rockland restaurant. It's only a few acres, this representative of the locavore movement, but I'm pleased to see any victory in the battle against lawns.

Harbour Hill Drive is much like Bayside, only wealthier. I don't get to the end of this one either. I leave it mid-way in and hurry away. There's a wood nearby; its coolness calls. What I had glanced at as I walked south a couple of hours ago – a two-track dirt road disappearing into trees – has suddenly become a compelling necessity. I need a purge, I need to find a hidden gem. And walking – not driving – finds it for me. I must have missed this track a thousand times, speeding in a car to the stores of Rockland.

The track gradually ascends up Ingraham's Hill between Harbour Hill and Freedom, and I walk for almost a mile without seeing house or lawn or loon-shaped mailbox. The owner of these woods (it's one person, I've learned, owning two sections of 80 acres each) has kept his sense, apparently, or maybe hasn't had the right offer, or (these days) any offer at all. The woods are fresh and my energy flows back and I suspect the track will come out eventually on the mysterious Weskeag marshes that I've not yet seen.

But for the third time I don't make it to the end of the road. My suburban soul feels the faintest frisson (fresh tire tracks in the mud, for example) of trespassing on someone else's wilderness, or perhaps I need to save the illusion of endlessness for another day. Or maybe lunch is conveniently calling. Nevertheless, here has survived a much better vision of life than the temerity of the Drives: a tangle of trees and shrubs, un-exhausted air, wanton weeds, puddles in the track, birds calling and leaves rustling, the quiet sound of land that is not silence, not noise.

There are even two metaphors made flesh. At the side of the track, ten minutes in, a rusty wreck of a car lies in the scrub, very old by the size of the wheels and the Model-T shape of the body, and then, a few steps on, a bald eagle takes flight in a flurry and a crashing – these two greatest symbols of America, one derelict and destructive, one very much alive and free, at least for a while.

There's one last trial, Freedom Drive. The houses here are the newest and biggest and the lots are the largest and almost every lot remains unsold. In fact, only three houses grace this half-mile of road. It's a place almost completely barren of trees, whether naturally or by bulldozer, and not only that, one of the three houses is missing the usual fringe of ornamental shrubs and lawn like Astroturf, and it stands there stark and naked like a model house hastily tarted up for a show. I feel judgments rising like crows from a field. The place announces, "Protect us from nature and unpleasantness, separate us from those unlike us." If that is the motivation, I will not hesitate to snipe and screech. Who builds on the tops of hills anyway but the well-to-do and insecure?

Yet what is here displayed may be the deepest American dream – freedom to be all by yourself, in luxury, dependent on others only at the remove of money – and it is one that I myself have strived for, that I suffer and enjoy every day. From an outside standpoint, I'm just as guilty of excess as any resident of Freedom Drive. Just the basics of living in two places make for embarrassment, however much I worry about my gas mileage and my electric meters and my roomfuls of stuff. And things get more confused. I'm well-steeped in the Calvinist talent for hypocritical criticism of others, and I might wish to employ it at the moment but for the annoying fact that if I ever got to know any of the people living here, to understand their problems and hopes and worries, I wouldn't be able to judge them at all. A person met singly will almost never fit a stereotype. (I reserve a couple of exceptions – bosses – from my past.)

And so the dilemmas and the divides grow bigger all the time, between individual and group, city and suburb, heaven and hell. Worldwide, some one billion of us are well off to degrees that range from the comfortable to the obscene. For the planet to survive as we know it, our lives must be changed – in degrees that range from simple education to profound regulation – for what if the other six billion people who don't live like this suddenly did? Who could blame them?

I should say at this point that I use the suburbs as a kind of straw man. I set them up to be destroyed, all the while knowing that many (well, a certain kind anyway) are pleasant, even beautiful. America invented them for a reason – they satisfy any number of personal and family needs. I have lived in one ever since settling down near Boston, 25 years in the same house no less, and continue to do so in my current, sometimes tenuous split between city and country, and my children knew nothing else but one suburban home, in a safe and loving neighborhood, until they went to college.

I can sit on my Massachusetts patio, under the big trees in the backyard, and dream almost as vividly as I can in Maine. There are deer in my suburb, and coyotes. A female wild turkey pecked away under our bird feeder recently, trailed by six little ones. I hardly have to mention the proliferation of rabbit and chipmunk and mouse and opossum and raccoon and of course the ubiquitous squirrel. A black bear wanders through Brookline, a moose is spotted in Concord. Thoreau would be beside himself – Maine has come to Massachusetts.

Of course, this is a matter of wildlife adapting to us and not vice versa. We're not adapting at all. We're mostly taking.

We will need time to fix the mess we've made, and probably don't have it. Places like Freedom Drive, not to mention my own good fortune, ought to be levied a carbon tax all their own. I *will* judge our collective behavior.

This is dispiriting stuff, and for the fourth time I don't complete the walk to the end of the line. Everything is all mixed up. Personally, one never seems to get to the end of anything, but collectively the end rushes at us like the apocalypse. Prophets are petted like house cats, profits are revered like gods. I walk back down the hill for the last time, and I can see in the short distance, just over the border into Rockland, the Victorian edifice of Primo, one of the best restaurants in the Northeast, where dinner for two costs a week's wages for someone from Everett Lane, and I see the shining waters of Penobscot Bay, and the faint outline of Vinalhaven, and a glimpse of the open sea – all the things you'd put on the Freedom brochure.

But at the same time, equally visible from this compromised Eden, I can see the warehouses and factories of Rockland Industrial Park, the squat, rusty, corrugated sheds of the Mid-Coast School of Technology, the little saltboxes down the hill. I can hear the traffic on Route 1. In too many places the changes have happened, maybe inevitably, and that's hard to accept. Our children may still have some certainties of forest and marsh and deep, pure, mysterious ocean to hold onto, but their children?

I retreat to the car. One last task: drive to ends of each Drive and therefore complete the mission, sort of. The car has broiled in the sun and I open all the windows to let in the sea breeze. I was the only walker on these streets today, and as I drive I review myself walking up and down, hot and tired but at least outside. People perhaps wondered who the crazy guy was. Nobody walks on such streets. Everything is too far away, stores and friends and your kids' play dates in the next development and maybe even the mailbox at the end of your driveway. Everybody drives. Visitors, authorized and not, reach the end of your street and it is dead, a circular cul de sac made to get into and out of without stopping. It's much easier not to think in a car, comfortable and anonymous and air-conditioned, glassed-in like a sun porch from flies and fresh air.

And now the car takes me away to my own house and deck, my own Eden where, away from the traps of the past and the worries of the future, I'll eat a sandwich and watch the eiders dive and make notes and read a book and for a while think about things industrial hardly at all.

North Shore Drive

It's late September now. Still hot. On successive mornings I'm walking the north side of Owls Head peninsula, the first walk from Central School more or less eastward and the second from Owls Head General Store more or less westward, each starting point chosen mostly as a convenient place to park the car, my accomplice on these walks.

It being a Sunday, the only people at the school are two women smoking cigarettes at a picnic table and their kids playing on the swings and jungle gym. Owls Head Central is a plain white rectangle built (obviously before the advent of school architects) in 1952, when consolidation closed all of the one-room schools. At one time Owls Head boasted six of them. Only two of those buildings remain, both re-purposed. The other four have vanished.

One thinks of such things with nostalgia, in the distant and irretrievable past, but like millions of Americans, I myself am only one degree of separation from that simpler time. My parents as children in Minnesota attended one-room schools; somehow every time they walked to school it was winter, at 30 below, a blizzard blowing, uphill both ways. My father actually started one in Cleveland, of the religious variety, at the beginning of his peripatetic career. This is no place to jump into the education controversy (big schools, little ones, same-sex, charter, mixed-grade, private, not to mention standardized testing), or into the peripeteia of one-room schools for that matter, but perhaps this experience of my parents rubbed off on me, because the thought of scores of children walking all over Owls Head to and from their local schools is a lovely one. Now we have buses, lots of buses, and perhaps more in the future.

The trends in education here are relentlessly modern. Owls Head centralized all elementary grades in 1952, was itself centralized a few years ago into Regional School Unit 13, offering only grades four through six, and now may be closed because of dwindling enrollment and the state's current budgetary disdain for education. School websites tout competition, through sports, technology, and test scores (which must ever increase) such that students even in rural Maine "will be trained for the global marketplace." Charter schools and academies and online learning companies seeking profits promote class divisions. When will we know what we're losing?

Generalists (and generalities) are certainly suspect now. Everyone is deemed to deserve a chance at college. And by "class" divisions I don't mean the schoolroom variety, I mean the widening gulf between peoples in almost any human endeavor you can think of, riches, religion, education, political philosophies – a gap that I expect to see firsthand on my walks this weekend. It must have been hard to be uppity in a one-room schoolhouse.

Before I make my way from the school toward North Shore Drive, I backtrack along Ash Point a bit to walk Woodman's Road, which is indeed wooded for a while, but which quickly ends in a trailer park. I stop at the edge, wary as a deer. A dozen mobile homes are parked on treeless lots. It is dead quiet in the burning sun. I see no movement, not even a stray cat. Here is represented one kind of settlement, one end of the wealth spectrum, in contrast with the rich ghettos I'll see on the north shore of the peninsula. Do birds of a feather stick together? Short of interviewing every resident from here to Garthgannon Road, I'll never know. It appears that way. I *can* say that in the 1990s my parents, in their difficult trajectory from very poor to reasonably comfortable, retired to a mobile home in the exurbs of Portland, decamping in the summers for Unity Pond farther north, and I do know that the scorn which people exhibit even in their pronunciation of the phrase "trailer park" is hardly justified. The sneerers wouldn't know anyone in such places, and that of course is the great flaw in our society, not to mention my own Owls Head travels, that we're thoroughly partitioned from the way other people live. Our judgments on their lives are made on very shaky ground. Caveat lector.

The intersection of Ash Point and North Shore Drives features a stark vision of the class divide. On one side of the road a horse farm has recently been converted into the Breakwater Vineyard (yes, a vineyard in Maine, and hardly the only one), and its southern-style manse sits high on its hill, flashing its white pillars and offering wine tastings on summer weekends. On the other side, on the down side, a tiny white building not much larger than a shed sits without a sign and hardly a purpose anymore. It's one of the old schoolhouse buildings still surviving, now in its third life: the death of the Head of Bay School became the birth of the Owls Head Grange in 1938; the death of the Grange in the 80s became the birth of a place (still locally known as Grange Hall) for pie and craft sales by the ladies of the Mussel Ridge Historical Society, some of whom look ancient enough to have gone to school in this very place and who are raising money to restore it. They probably say the words "Central School" through gritted teeth.

I'd like to see the inside but the door is locked, and my inspection will have to await next summer's Grange Sale. Buy a blueberry pie and a tea cosy; drive up the hill for a glass of Riesling.

Now to North Shore Drive. Other North Shores I've known, in Chicago and Boston, imply a certain elegance, or at least the lots get bigger and the houses newer and grander the further you get from the city or the closer you get to the water. It seems to be true here as well. Here at the drive's beginning, the 18th and 19th centuries are plainly seen in the white houses along the road, inhabited by the old, the poor or the simply-minded, but their properties are inevitably bisected by right-of-ways, long lanes and driveways going down the several hundred yards to the shore, where quite different animals live. The shore denizens like the comforts: their houses are new and large and their lots big and grassy, and what trees there are have been pruned into small clumps so as not to spoil the view of Rockland Harbor.

I walk down Sherman's Lane, which appears to be a public road, more or less. The view of Rockland fits my general mood of gap analysis, for it is both lovely and ugly, if that can be. In the foreground the blue water of the bay is speckled with boats. In the middle ground a cement factory looms in Rockland itself, and on the city's waterfront a huge old plant that used to process herring for sardines now boils seaweed into carrageenan. In the background rise the blue-green, other-worldly eminences of the Camden Hills.

I walk down the next lane where our 200 years of "progress" are painfully evident in just one property, called Smith's Cottages. A large old farmhouse very much in need of paint borders North Shore Drive, and lace curtains and a Subaru wagon from the 90s suggest the proprietors of those cottages are in habitation; a series of former chicken barns mostly falling down, with no paint left at all, provided their income at one time; three cute, brightly and differently painted A-frame cottages for rent near the shore do so now; and actually on the shore rise some suburban Colonials. I imagine various Smiths over the years trying to keep up with material progress, or out of bankruptcy, one often leading to the other, by selling their shoreline to flatlanders.

On the other side of North Shore Drive, the 20th century as usual announces itself with housing developments, but less pretentiously than on Ingraham's Hill. One of these new roads is unashamedly called LMNOP Drive, and I'm still trying to figure out that derivation. Another, Oak Run, sounds more traditional, until I think of "run" as a verb – and don't you wish trees could just pick up and leave our depredations. That name too must go on the list, one that already includes streets nearer to home, Gigi's Place, Mimilou's Way, and Itsocosy (sic).

And that's one of the things I love about Maine: the frankly sentimental next to the serious, the corny and naïve deliberately embraced, the calculated countrifications. You're never quite sure what the next corner, or day, or revisit will bring, and when I get home to retrace my steps on Google Maps, there's a further delight for the list. Apparently (for I saw no sign), LMNOP has an extension. Naturally, it's QRS Drive.

****

Monday morning is another hot one, and I start my second walk along North Shore Drive at its eastern end, at the general store in Owls Head village, and will work westward. The car's technically not in the store's parking area (it's parked across the road at the pond), but patrons and proprietor alike may wonder what it's doing there all morning. And would they get it if I explained what I'm doing? He's walking the roads of Owls Head? What for? It still seems odd to me too, doing something so obviously "from away," driving the car to take a walk, something faintly embarrassing, as if I were an author or something. A walk is something you do from your doorstep. Writing is something you do for money. Driving a car needs a real purpose. Strike three.

I walk the south side of the drive going out, and the north side, the water side, coming back, to save the "good" side and its lanes down to the ocean for last. Not that the south side isn't wonderful. Almost the whole road is bordered by the deep woods of the interior of Owls Head peninsula. Soon enough I see a trail into the trees, and it takes some willpower not to leave the road forthwith, to trade hard and noisy macadam for birdsong and the soft springiness of pine needles. Those trees stand with open arms, massed together, lovely as sylphs, their almost 800 acres of road-lessness beckoning to the wanderer, and their embrace would feel like a lover's hug. But they will be there to call another day; today, I must view a few more puny developments (such as The Oak That Runs) that poke into the pelt of the woods like porcupine quills. (I wish the woods could shake itself hard and flip them away.)

North Shore Drive is hilly and curvy here, with an occasional glimpse of water. It's still a country road, but an improved one. It's not like the other places I've walked: a trail in the woods, quiet and peaceful; a narrow two-track dirt road, with weeds and puddles, fairly rare in these civilized days; a suburban drive, with berms; or a lane, dirt or tarred, built for access to houses that prefer to be widely scattered, and affording views of woods and fields and sea only occasionally interrupted by the automobile, and then it's usually a car belonging to a resident. North Shore Drive's upgrade to a real road is a necessity. It's the road that most tourists take to get to the end of the peninsula, where Owls Head Lighthouse State Park sits like an emerald sanctuary, and the traffic is sufficient to warrant fresh pavement every couple of years and double yellow lines its entire length. Such a road can still be beautiful, but its pretty views contrasting with noise and speed is a little disconcerting. Not dangerous for pedestrians, mind you, not really. The speed limit is on the low side, and the great majority of drivers do not try to pick you off as you walk the narrow shoulder.

Walking here does give me a chance to analyze rural driving behavior. I particularly note the amount of space that vehicles allow for safety. Some drivers coming at me move completely over the double yellow into the opposite lane. Some more or less straddle it, still providing plenty of room. A few, just a few, make the minimum effort, adjusting the steering wheel by a millimeter or two to give me the maximum rush of air and exhaust, perhaps even intentionally. Maybe I could do some kind of study to account for these varying degrees of courtesy, a study related to sex and age of driver, kind of vehicle, state of registration....But I'm without a notebook, and even these small numbers of variables are too much to hold in the brain at once, and while perhaps I'd like to tell you that research proves the closest shaves are administered by young men driving pick-ups from Massachusetts, I just can't control the data.

After some 15 minutes of fruitless brain work, I chide myself for ignoring this beautiful day. It's so easy to focus on the ugly and the incongruous, like the billions of useless automobile trips we make every day, so easy to retreat into numbers, or daydreams, or get-rich-quick schemes to assuage anxiety. How much better it is just to smile and wave at the drivers for their kindness on the yellow-lane road, and to take pleasure in the simple movement of the limbs. How much better to know this *is* the Emerald City, you've already reached it, and the proof is in the stunning autumn flowers, the cool deep woods, the glimpse or two of Penobscot Bay, and even in the shining blue-and-silver can of Red Bull fallen in the ditch like a patch of sky.

Walking west, I give Deerfield Lane and Toy Box Lane (list!) a miss because they look like private driveways, possibly with dogs. But then I reach North Shore Woods Drive, a real road too obvious to be ignored. When I first walk in, there's a road crew at the end of the drive just breaking for lunch, and I suppose I become flustered, having to pass so close and say hello to three men spattered with tar and shutting down large machines and looking at me like the locals usually do, friendly enough (one older fellow with a large white beard comments to me on the niceness of the day) but also reserved (the other two kind of smile and murmur something and don't quite meet my eyes). And so the strangeness of the houses on the drive doesn't register.

They look varied enough at first glance, just another subdivision. But then I look more closely and realize that, in spite of different roof styles and even the addition of half-stories here and there, all the houses, at least a dozen of them spread down a quarter mile of road, started off with the same blueprint. They were all little boxes, an unmistakable scent of the 50s. When I was a kid, I lived in one like this for a few years, when my family first moved to the exurbs of Grand Rapids, Michigan.

5115 Mildred Avenue was just like every other house on the street, and Mildred was pretty much like Blaine Avenue and Southglow Court, cul-de-sacs converted from farmland, and when I visited it 50 years later the houses looked much as I remembered except there are now some trees. The area, however, changed immensely. In 1955 Mildred Street was practically in the country. Corn grew in the fields behind the house. But the rich soil of Western Michigan succumbed to asphalt and lawns, and in 2008 a large condo development crowded up to old Mildred's back, and mini-malls sprouted everywhere.

Americans wanted to be all the same after the war. They craved safe uniformity. They had suffered the Depression, and fascists, and those who survived worked hard and long to achieve peace. The land of western Michigan, flat, treeless, fit right in. It was perfect for efficient, conforming development and suffered spectacularly as a result. (And perhaps its spirit did too – that house on Mildred can be had for as little as $75,000.) But individuality grew as wealth did, and now we want to be different. Or do we? We still seem to clump together by class and race, our dreams are still driven by what we see on screens. At least here on North Shore Woods Drive, the developers kept the trees and large lots and the residents put money and ideas in their dwellings (are trees and creativity related?). Most important, there is no large city nearby to pressure the woods.

The strangeness of North Shore Woods Drive is most evident at its end. Picture a large lot, cleared, with a scraggly lawn, a couple of tricycles standing around, woods in back. Picture a ranch house in the middle of the lot, plain and unadorned, but it's not just one house, it's a double one. Two ranches are stuck together lengthwise, mirror images, sharing an end wall between them. It's as if the developers reached the end of their possibilities and tried to maximize their profits. Not a double-wide mobile home but a double-long stationary one. As I said, Maine is full of wonders.

I regain the main road, reach Oak Doing the 400, give it a short look (it's unremarkable), and turn around to walk east. Little lanes start to trickle down to the water in the usual fashion. At the end of Windswept Way, given the fancy name and the lack of development, I expect some mansion at its end. I'm greeted with a small trailer parked under trees, almost a camper. On Post Lane the owners of the nice houses on the water must drive through a marine junkyard to get to them, a most incredible collection of at least a dozen stranded boats, hundreds of lobster traps and buoys, bait barrels and fish trays strewn everywhere, old tires, ancient motors, innumerable coils of rope – a place worthy of the artistic attention of a Rosamund Purcell devoted to the ocean. At the start of Cooper's Beach Road, a man and woman are re-shingling a house, and in my Maine bubble of romance, I'm pleased to imagine it's a husband-wife team working together, something you'd seldom see in the city.

Farther down the same road, I see on a lawn what looks at first glance like a haphazard arrangement of wire lobster traps, a common decoration even in semi-suburbia. On second glance, and I do get a second glance, since I'm walking and not driving, I see order and plan. About 10 traps have been laid end-to-end in a row on the grass, and a few more lead up some porch steps to the house. In the middle of the row, two traps are stacked vertically and contain what looks like a tree of sticks. A kind of pet run, I think.

On the return trip up the lane, I pass the traps again and as if on cue, a house cat dutifully trots out of the house, down the steps, to the end of the run. Inside the traps, of course; the ends have been removed to make this catwalk. I don't care to embarrass the Persian in its little wilderness, so I don't stand around to see if it also jumps into its faux jungle gym, whose stick tree I now see is hung with objects to bat.

And I thought helicopter parents guarded only humans. All children can get a taste of the great outdoors without any danger. Frightening woods are all around, after all, and upon one's loose pet or young son might spring a tick, a weasel, a fisher, a marten, a bear. A pick-up might bear down, or indeed pick up. And when they become teenagers we'll send them into the world protected by wire cages made of cell phones and birth control and GPS and credit cards. They'll escape danger by a quick flick of plastic.

I leave these half-suburban places and head for the more expansive neighborhoods to the east. I'm now about half-way to the promised land at the end of the peninsula, and I've crossed some kind of invisible line, clearly. There are now no houses directly on North Shore Drive, just trees giving shelter from the riff-raff. By the time I'm just a few yards down Dynamite Beach Road I can hear no traffic noise. The woods here haven't been logged for a while; they give the impression of depth and tranquility. No houses yet: we're still far from the water. But at the first lane off Dynamite, called Torney, near the communal tennis court, I see a symbol so perfect for this part of Owls Head that I could be accused of making it up. Attached to a pole, next to a large basket of flowers, made of metal is a yard-high dollar sign.

I've thought about this semiotically ("the new totem God"), crudely ("You need serious money to live here, bub"), rationally (must be part of something else now fallen down, since it's so rusty), but I don't get it. I can't imagine the motivation (or don't want to) to put up such a potent symbol, except as a joke. Maybe it is. The impression of someone with a sense of humor is reinforced by a large, somewhat messy house a little farther down the lane, where I see a realtor's sign that says, "Not for Sale." But that dollar sign: crude or silly, intended or ironic, the message is pretty clear.

At least the houses of Dynamite Beach are tasteful. This is not true, in my humble opinion, of the houses along Weeks Road, the next development. The woods are just as generous and the lots just as large, but from nice New England farmhouses and capes and their impression of verticality, we move to the horizontal: new houses longer than higher, bigger too, some covered in siding, some in clapboards painted, not stained, no bare and weathered cedar shakes as on Dynamite, trees removed in favor of lawns, straight driveways, shrubs rather than bushes, a flatness of landscape, a place tamed rather than accepted.

I expect I read too much into these things. I expect that I'm wrong to believe that people who preserve trees and respect natural tradition are liberal in all other things as well. I expect that the visual impression given by a neighborhood doesn't necessarily determine who means to buy there. But to my way of thinking, the people of Dynamite Beach are conservative in the old sense of the word, and the people of Weeks Road are conservative in its current, political sense, and it shows in their houses. I feel like some kind of amateur sociologist precariously defining groups, but I'm compelled by all the neighborhoods I've seen today to say that class gradations in America are as numerous as in any European country, and we betray them not by our speech and our history but by our possessions. Americans look outward and forward, anxiously so. The past has nothing to say, and I can't help but think that the people of Weeks Road, wealthy themselves, still gaze enviously across Broad Cove at the really rich people on the other side.

****

Thus, one more walk for this chapter. When I planned these walks, I thought that my North Shore visit would end at Weeks Road, and that the last "neighborhood" between Weeks and the lighthouse belonged more logically to the village. It doesn't. The village is old and modest and a real neighborhood, none of which describes this last walk in what amounts to a museum collection of very large houses, discreetly scattered.

It's now half-way through October. The weather has at last cooled. It's a shorter walk today, just three lanes off Lighthouse Road, two of them different in degree from the likes of Weeks

51

and Dynamite but still more or less the same in kind, and the last, Garthgannon Road, quite different again. Broad Cove and Tote Roads show the usual pattern, just wealthier: long "driveways" through woods, large houses at the end on the shore. House numbers are placed on tasteful rocks, on a fancy light post, or even on small stone pillars. But only Garthgannon actually has stone pillars, large ones, guarding its entrance, looking as it could be chained off if necessary; only Garthgannon is lined by no utility poles or wires (How do they do that? Run them underground? For a mile?); only Garthgannon has a double tennis court; only Garthgannon ends in houses large enough to mimic a kind of Shaker Heights or Chestnut Hill on the bay. It's far beyond me to understand why people need so much room in what probably are second, or even third houses.

If I'm honest, it's not completely beyond me. It's as if people need to insulate themselves against the world as largely and massively as possible, to re-create their own world in mimicry of the vastness of the universe. I understand this desire to shelter and shield, if that's all it is. But when it's mixed with greedy ostentation, I must protest.

The great irony of Garthgannon Road is not only that it is named after a modest tourist lodge that stood on the shore in the 19th century, but that the lodge was sold in 1904 to the missionary-like Bancroft School. I found online a little book called *Book of Views*, published in 1916 by the Bancroft Training School of Haddonfield, New Jersey. Margaret Bancroft founded the school there in 1883 and purchased Garthgannon as a summer home in Maine for her students, children with "physical infirmities and retard (sic) mental growth." There are pictures in New Jersey of the gymnasium, the manual training room, and the sense training room with its menagerie of people puppets and stuffed animals, including a child-sized elephant, its line-up of geometrical objects, its potted ferns, and (perhaps for the wealthy parents) a large scale-model sailing yacht. There are pictures in Owls Head of the lodge, of the bathing beach where the students are carefully attended in the water by teachers in full bathing attire, and a romantic view of "the harbor at twilight." The Bancroft still exists in New Jersey, but apparently there was retrenchment in 1998 and the property in Maine was sold to a developer from Boston.

The biggest house in the development now called Ocean Edge is for sale, for only $3.25 million. It's at least the third time on the market in ten years, retreating in price each time. It's a dwelling not only three stories high but elongated beyond comprehension, as if to keep family members or guests as far from each other as possible. The pictures on the realtor's website show an interior stuffed with vaguely Victorian furniture and statues and sconces and vases without end. Every edge seems gilded or scalloped. If there was an empty space of more than 6 square feet, the owner has filled it with a table or a shelf, and stacked the table and shelf with a lamp, a curio, an arrangement of white candles, a cloisonné tray, and the tray with pretty stones. I didn't see any books. Here are the over-ripe fruits of several industrial revolutions. Outside, the lawns are trimmed right down to the high-tide mark, the driveways impeccably graveled, the trees and shrubs shaped each season. And I expect that Margaret Bancroft's "harbor at twilight" has become mostly a backdrop for the cocktail set, Androids to hand, for lavish parties on patios, for wide lawns and gazebos and concrete piers and all the other things that accessorize the lives of the rich.

That this extravaganza borders an old and modest village is one thing. That it exists less than two miles from that oddly moving 2-family ranch, and just three miles from the trailer park, is an indictment of a system.

Like most people, I'm curious about the lives of the rich. Do they suffer like me with every market downturn, clutching their investment statements in agony? Maybe not the very rich like Mr. and Mrs. Victoriana, who are perhaps retreating from five houses to four, or like those financial wizards who get richer shorting the sufferings of others. But the chances are that even they do worry, for in order to gain and advance and keep a position, one has to acquire a certain way of looking at the world, especially if one earned wealth from business. In my experience, businessmen tend to believe that the world is full of devious people all competing and negotiating and desperate to rule, full of objects to be bought, existing for pecuniary pleasure. Thus in consequence may I present their huge protected spaces, the manicured taming of nature, the restlessness of mansions.

The complicating factor, of course, is that rich people are often generous with their fortunes. The existence of land trusts, for example, depends on just that.

Some time after this particular walk, I met the owners of one of the houses of Ocean Edge. They are lovely people, and support many causes, including the land trust I volunteer for, with both time and money, and their house is large but spare and respectful of the land. It's the other rich – the strivers, the ambitious, the greedy – that I can't help condemning, those that apparently have no conscience at all; worse, they are the new idols of our society. And if that ostentatious pile eating up the shore actually represents not the truly rich at all but a series of over-extended wannabes, whose dreams of getting away from it all were as short-lived and stupid as they were impossible, then shame on us (and me) for peeping at them like a voyeur, for still wanting what they have and thinking that people like me would use those resources for the good of the land.

"A man is rich in proportion to the things he can afford to let alone," Thoreau wrote. Good advice, but it's from a saint. The rest of us find it extremely difficult not to be envious of the rich, even though we have a thousand times more stuff and money than Thoreau ever had. (Remember, this is from someone who has a house, albeit a modest one, at the end of a lane.) We can't leave it alone. Why do we want a million times more?

It's all very well to fantasize that my stewardship of such wealth would be different, but it probably wouldn't. I too would spend slightly beyond my means for the bigger house, on a rocky point, surrounded by a score of acres protecting me and my family from pain and worry and fellow needy humans. At all levels of wealth we spend and hoard. It's just the methods that differ.

The North Shore of Owls Head thus represents all walks of life. All of us, at every class level, walker or driver, want our view of the world to be right. The imperative is to be responsible in some way, whatever your means. That will make the difference between people happy and people desperate, between money that makes people less secure, more divorced from nature, and money that restores and preserves, between a sustainable planet and a dying one.

As I walk back to the old, plain village, I envision the development on North Shore Drive over the last hundred years as a compressed, 5-minute video. It would show a tide of civilization advancing inexorably eastward. Subdivisions burst out, woods disappear into sinkholes, roads suddenly ooze with tar, lodges explode and mansions pop like pimples, and it all comes to an abrupt and welcome halt at the green bulwark of Owls Head Lighthouse State Park against which progress can advance no farther.

Village

Owls Head village is a modest place. A few dozen houses straggle along roads and shore. There's almost no commerce, and no grand row of captain's houses lines Main Street as in other seaside towns in Maine, neighboring Thomaston, for example. Although some 40 captains did live here, they were quiet men, trading with the sea, not the Far East, and their houses had little pretense. Neither was there much shipbuilding, usually the other genesis of wealth on the coast, although there was a flurry of activity in the mid-19th century, when the government improved the harbor and a couple of frigates and a schooner were built. Today's residents do seem to make their living from the sea, judging by more than 30 lobster boats in the harbor, but that's hardly a source of wealth as we know it today. There are almost no mansions or estates; those who don't live by the lobster live by retirement checks.

Nor is the village an old place, at least by the standards of New England. Although Champlain discovered the promontory in 1605, the plague of white people didn't arrive until the early 18th century. In 1764, there were only four houses in all of Owls Head, and those were mostly farmsteads down the road on Ash Point. A rural outpost of Thomaston and South Thomaston for many years, the village didn't start to coalesce until the 19th century, as the industrializing country brought leisure time and a desire for the seaside to the masses.

The village is hardly densely populated. Houses stand quite far apart. There aren't any row houses or tenements or dormitories, for there were no granite, textile or other processing industries to attract the poor. Indeed, the sum total of non-residence establishments is as follows: the post office, the general store, the Baptist church, the library (open Wednesday evenings, "weather permitting," and Saturdays "9:00 - 5:00-ish"), and two lobster dealers, Ship to Shore and Owls Head

Lobster, although as I walk through town, the suggestion of a former store catches my eye. Propped up against the decaying wall of a two-story shed on a side street are hand-painted signs that say "The Personal Book Store," perhaps a reminder of the fact that Owls Head, especially Crescent and Holiday Beaches just to the south, used to be a resort for the rising middle class. If that shed had been the store itself, then it's been falling down for many decades. The signs, however, look somewhat younger (some misguided city romantic attempted a resurrection?), as does the usual Maine collection of junk in the yard, among which is a briefcase standing upright, the vinyl, rectangular, hard-sided kind that businessmen in the 50s used to carry, full of their important papers and large enough to bring their offices not only home but on vacation as well, at a time when the family came to the coast for the summer and the bread-winner joined them when he could.

The tide of city tourists seeking sun and shore and dances and afternoon teas did not strike Owls Head village all that hard, and had few lasting effects. Owls Head Inn on the harbor, now a private residence, was well-known, and the beaches along South Shore Drive attracted many visitors from Boston and New York, but greater numbers came from Rockland and central Maine. It remained largely a middle-class colony, home-grown. But then in 1921 Owls Head successfully separated from South Thomaston, and got its fair share of taxes for schools and road improvement, and very quickly became a bedroom community for Rockland and a haven of second-homers from places south. The automobile had changed a culture again. No more organized sociability: now the village is mostly a destination for list-checkers ("Owls Head Lighthouse – got it, only 10 more to go this trip") and travel website addicts ("Owls Head General Store serves the best hamburgers in Maine") and escapees from the city and, oh yes, those few dozen lobstermen, roaring to sea at 5:00 a.m. and drinking too much and working harder than Hercules and retreating to their small houses in the affordable places not on the shore, semi-consciously providing the "local color" that brings the list-checkers to Maine in the first place.

It's always fascinating to walk through town and see the shiny Volvos mixing it up with the battered pick-ups. Not too many of the former today; it's a blustery November noon, well past tourist season, and although there are quite a few cars at the general store, they carry Maine plates. I tell myself this would be a good time to try that famous hamburger and meet some locals, but characteristically, I park the car at the pond and walk down Lighthouse Road to the state park. After the walk, perhaps.

It's a beautiful walk, a lovely mixture of town and country. Several large white houses line a low ridge up from the road and the shore; the shore is occupied with the weirs and piers and stacks of traps of the two lobster companies; and in between, bisected by the road, are great grassy fields, periodically cut for hay, acres of prime views of the harbor and the islands, not developed. Someone is protecting a grand way of life, remnants of a saltwater farm, perhaps.

How fragile that protection is! A death, uninterested heirs, aggressive developers – and the fields are gone.

The small town way of life can be a joy or a penance or both, but I worry most of all about its vulnerability. Masses of people in cities destroy things, but they can also organize to protect them, for example, by checking the favoritism or self-interest of selectmen on a zoning board. In the towns on the Maine coast, so many zoning decisions seem to favor the tourist trade that quaintness is inevitable. When we first came to Owls Head in 1995, Rockland just five miles to the north featured gritty bars and stores selling hardware and marine supplies. Now its Main Street has aspirations, with shops (Fiore Artisan Olive Oils and Vinegars!) and galleries and high-end restaurants, and soon it will be indistinguishable from Bar Harbor, Camden, and Boothbay. Will our quiet little town be next? Quick development is unlikely - there are no big attractions. But the open spaces of town could gradually fill in, and the natives will be pushed out.

The lobstermen already have to commute from a distance just like any office worker.

Perhaps this is why I get an almost visceral reaction against any kind of new building, not just the obvious Walmart or Dunkin Donuts, but also a house going up in a woodlot. The bare wood of rafters screams in pain; the fox that hunted here retreats if it can, if it can find a den somewhere else; the soil is gashed into mud and dreads the mono-culture lawn to come. I feel slightly insane at these times, caught in irrationality. In 1924 my own house, then a cottage, was built on a one-time woodlot. My own life endlessly and dangerously consumes. I am one of billions. Yet I don't want more people. I want more nature. How much is love of nature just the selfish desire to avoid people?

What I really mean, I think, is that the human need to conquer nature is becoming more and more distasteful to me. New houses go up in the modern way of construction – buy big lot, knock down all trees, build large house (large trending to huge: there are no small houses being built around here) – and I have to think there is little admirable about the enterprise. There's no attempt to fit with the landscape. It will have a gourmet kitchen that's seldom cooked in. Did the owner think about buying an existing place and rehabbing? Such a house is far too big for the two people who will probably live in it. It's a symbol of our need for ease and comfort at all cost. It's a symbol of our fear of nature and its unpredictability. Build big to carve out a protective space. Manicure your lawn, plant your gardens with all manner of non-native plants. When did this need to conquer nature evolve? We killed for meat, not for sport. Didn't we used to merge into nature, into beauty? Now we insulate as much as possible, as if to deny our fragility.

Of course life is fragile. It always has been. Nature demonstrates that not only in storms and earthquakes and disease, but in its very essence. The seasons are a constant parade of birthing and dying, but in the new and sterile way of living, the human goal is to be season-less, air-conditioned. I expect that makes people less human, or at least makes them deny their inescapable genetic ties to nature. What a recipe for unhappiness, aggression, war, greed. If we deny our place in the world, we are all the more easily led around, nose-ringed, by politicians, religious pretenders, or personal selfishness.

It sounds trivial, but I'm going to say it anyway. How about a walk along a pretty shore, through a city park, or on conservation land? While not everyone is so lucky to have a bit of wilderness nearby, everyone has access to a tree. Even a weed can be beautiful if you take it to heart. Everything natural that you experience should be like a podcast, titled "your genes at work."

****

On my grumpy village walk this day, I'm lucky to have Owls Head Light State Park nearby. I walk through the gates and see the mass of spruce and immediately feel better. My pretensions and obsessions and worries become slightly laughable. A body can be revived so easily.

There's no one in the park today but a couple of guys eating sandwiches in a utility truck, perfectly illustrating my point. Even the power company, a symbol of greed and development if there ever was one, needs a refuge.

The Owls Head promontory, the one the Micmac Indians named Mecadacut, was an obvious place to build a lighthouse. The gut between Owls Head harbor and Monroe Island is a narrow and dangerous one, and Rockland's growing lime industry at the turn of the 19th century required safe passage for the hundreds of ships transporting lime to cities south. The light was built in 1825, but its utilitarian value has now been diminished, like most lighthouses, in favor of its touristic value.

The walk from the parking lot follows the cliffs, and is just long enough, and close enough to the edge – it's a thrilling 75 feet down to sharp rocks and heavy surf – to wipe civilization from your mind. The keeper's house still stands after 150 years, but keepers are long banished by automation.

If you're lucky and visit on a summer weekend when Marla Haskins Rogers is docent, she'll tell you about living in the keeper's house as a child. Maybe she'll also tell you about the spirits that haunt the place, the mysterious footprints in the snow. Maybe she'll tell you about the frozen couple of Owls Head, Richard Ingraham and Lydia Dyer, whose ship ran aground in a terrible December storm in 1850, who were found encased in ice on the deck, who were thawed and massaged for two hours in the keeper's kitchen, and who lived to marry and have four children. But the views from the lens room at the top are so spectacular – all of Penobscot Bay opens in front of you – that you'll have trouble focusing on what she's saying.

I was so transfixed, and shy, that the one time I heard her talk, I could only think of mentioning that I lived just down the shore a ways. Was I trying to connect to the stories? To her? No, I was being a jerk from away.

Some of your fellow tourists will visit to add to their life lists, in which endeavor the United States Lighthouse Society aids and abets. Its Passport Program consists of four passport-style books that can be stamped at the lighthouses you visit, each book offering space for 60 stamps and each completed book earning an "official, collectible" embroidered round patch (for framing? Sewing on your sou'wester?). Your fourth and final book gets you to the highest level of achievement, the Platinum Circle Patch. But that isn't all. If the PCP isn't enough, if your lighthouse hunting becomes an obsession (there are nearly 700 in the US, after all), you can earn three more curved patches called Wings, also representing 60 lighthouses each, to be sewn around your Platinum Circle Patch, encircling it. I don't know how you survive after bagging 420; The World Lighthouse Society seems to offer no life-lister fixes.

I'm always amazed at the world of special interests. Lighthouses are of course dramatic symbols of time past or ships foundered or commerce traded or islands conquered or whatever your particular historical obsession may be. But something similar could be said of almost everything – knitting, the study of lichen, matchbox collections – and is a testament to another side of human creativity. We're not all development and ambition and soapboxes and the terrible thirst for possessions. Not all of our pursuits have to be loud. There are also these quiet passions, for the vagaries and oddballs of life. Give me car nuts over Jesus freaks any day.

But for whatever reason you're here at Owls Head Light State Park, I'm pleased that you can hardly avoid seeing the bay and the woods, listening to gulls and surf, and smelling the salty tang of air. Perhaps you'll also think of the people and the work that protect such places.

****

I return to the village and take the long way around back to my car, on Shell Street and then South Shore Drive. Shell Street hosts an odd house that I discover was called Castle Comfort, complete with battlements and crenellations, built by a Baptist minister as a summer place. It is presently being renovated, probably not by Baptists. The only other sign of religion in town, indeed on the whole peninsula, is Owls Head Baptist Church.

Later at home, I found online an informal history of said church, and between the lines of God-praise there are enough hints that the people of Owls Head in general were never terribly religious. In 300 years of European habitation only two churches were founded, a chapel here in the village which wasn't built until 1890 and one in the former Ash Point Village, built around the same time but which burned and wasn't replaced. And there was a constant shortage of ministers, except perversely in the summers when the population increase naturally included men of the cloth, when one could argue that religion was least needed, given the glories all around. Fortunately, most of these excess ministers seemed to be from away, vacationers or summer-home owners or professors from seminaries (including two in Massachusetts, Gordon Bible College and Newton Theological Seminary), and the townspeople probably wouldn't need to heed them even if they went to church.

This Massachusetts connection makes me think yet again of revisitation. I'm not religious, I should point out, but coming to Owls Head makes me at least think more about religious things. I wonder in particular if religious people who live in such a beautiful place are actually very religious at all. Prominent on the sign for the Baptist church, for example, is the kind message, "Help Us Help the Haitian Refugees." No sanctimonious or hectoring commands to obey, love, praise, repent, and believe as you might find on city church signs (sample in Rockland: "Go to church – don't wait for the hearse to take you"). I note too that Owls Head Baptist is quite small, really still a chapel, but is more than doubled in size by a two-story addition, seamlessly married to the worship space. Never in my extensive experience of churches have I seen a sanctuary debased by so secular an annex. It's plain and utilitarian and square; nothing points or soars heavenward. One of its levels is clearly the parsonage and the other a community center. Doctrine and rigorous worship, I suspect, are not the focus of this congregation.

Of course not: they already live in a state of grace, every day they see the marvels of God in woods and sea. And the more I visit, the more time I spend in Maine, I get it. It's when I go back to the city that knives are sharpened, guns are drawn, sects are at war. I actually become anti-religious.

Living closer to nature does not save me in the conventional sense. It's comforting and thrilling enough that I can entertain the possibility of the divine – He/She/It might exist – but there is no reason to believe or deny it. To be religious one has to be emotionally involved. You get poked by God, or you become insecure by upbringing, or your whole culture conspires to make you dependent. I've never experienced any of that, except perhaps at age 15, in the flat culture of central Minnesota, where my profession of faith was most likely some temporary and misplaced longing for love. But in a place like Owls Head, the emotional content becomes esthetic, or should I say that the unknowable becomes solid. I can revisit a goldfinch. The attributes people normally assign to a god are obvious if you just look around: there's no need to fight over the particulars.

Here the agony over the works of man and the guilt of God fades away. The human need to congregate in villages and churches and associations and bars can be taken at face value. It won't fester. Social and religious distortion occurs mostly when people are too crowded together, when they break connections to the land and the sea.

****

There's one last place to visit in the village – the junkyard of William Buckminster, a man who had protean connections to the land and sea and people of Maine. He's the eccentric that Rosamund Purcell wrote about in her book *Owls Head: On the Nature of Lost Things*. When she first met him in 1981 (she was attending the photography school in Rockport and came to Owls Head to shoot the lighthouse) he was well on his way to being an oddball. His wife had died in 1976 and his mooring to respectable life seemed to break. They had owned an antiques shop since the 50s and always had pack rat tendencies, and upon his wife's death those attributes became extreme; Bill turned his shop into a junkyard without equal. His 11 acres across from the general store were piled with every conceivable relic of 20th century civilization – foundry equipment, 15-foot stacks of window frames, oil tanks, lead plumbing, dinghies. Car bodies became storage bins. A hill of copper wire gleamed like a retirement account. Inside his barns there was an incredible chaos of furniture and ladders and metal sheeting, mostly unorganized, but then, there, a bin holds only a mass of the heroic figures detached from bowling trophies, and three cases display books swollen with dampness, mouse-infested, tattered.

In a way, the mountains of stuff were a natural outgrowth of Bill's many interests. He was a welder, a fish-cutter and -monger, a pool shark of national repute, an avid ice-skater and hockey fan, an antiques dealer, a man who lived in one place almost his whole life. His fellow Owls Headers tolerated him (except perhaps for the ladies of the Garden Club to whom the rusting, rotting mess was an abomination); people from away were alternately affronted and attracted; and Rosamund Purcell, already a photographer of some repute and soon to be called the "doyenne of decay," was transfixed. For more than 20 years she travelled to Owls Head and bought Bill's stuff, transporting it back to her Boston studios by the truckload, to be sorted and arranged and photographed.

A friend gave us her book shortly after it was published in 2003. I'm sorry to say I did not rush right out to experience Bill's ecstasy of junk. I could catch glimpses of the piles as we drove through the village, but its aspect was forbidding, and Buckminster had plastered the place with "No Trespassing" signs (odd for an antiques/junk seller), and I was still in my stressed out, uncurious, hide-me-away visiting state of mind. But today's revisitation of the village requires more exploration.

Eerily, there's nothing left. The notorious 11 acres are bare, returned to a nature of grasses and weeds and trees and shrubs. Buckminster had died in 2010 at 87, still eccentric, unmoveable until the last couple of frail years, and his family sold or cleared everything away. Nothing is left of him but an obituary online, and an artist's book, and Maine's famous and ferocious independence of land, even in the middle of a village. It's an extreme case to be sure, but emblematic of an attitude pervading the state. A man lives and fights and dies for his bit of heaven, but at the same time he doesn't much care what's on it. Trees, old washing machines, raspberry bushes, a collection of tires: the land is his to do with what he wants. No neatly edged lawns, no exotic shrubs carefully mulched, no garden sheds that look like dollhouses, no fancy weather vanes: a Maine man doesn't really care what others think. But amazingly enough, he's still tolerant of them, even the vacationers, the second-homers, the flatlanders who've been coming to Owls Head since the 19th century to sample its shores.

It's not just because we bring dollars. It's that our man is willing to give us the benefit of the doubt. Anyone who has the sense to come to Maine must be considered innocent of land-grabbing and culture-warping until proven otherwise. He is given a chance, without the fuss of religion or class, to be converted to the land and re-born.

South Shore

In the late 1800s a summer colony was founded on Crescent Beach. The cottages were modest to begin with, and a few of them, especially those on Ginns Point Road, seem to have survived to this day un-expanded, not gussied-up. The owners back then were not summer people from un-Maine but came from Rockland just a few miles up the coast, or perhaps from Augusta inland. They had a glorious, east-facing view, one that I imagine hasn't changed for centuries, providing you look not along the shore but out on the bay: the sparkling pure blue water; two little postage-stamp islands, Treasure and Emery, all rocks and firs, in the near distance; two bigger islands, Sheep and Monroe in the middle distance; in the far distance mythical Vinalhaven; and the open endless ocean to the south.

Leaving the car at home, I've already walked some three miles today, taking Ash Point Drive to its intersection with South Shore Drive and eventually reaching Crescent Beach. It's a warmish January Tuesday, with a huge changeable sky that went from sunny to cloudy to sunny in the 45 minutes it took to walk here, and I stand on the pebbles marveling at its immensity. No one is about. All the cottages, big and small, look deserted. After a few minutes a pickup comes along and parks. The driver looks through binoculars out to sea, as if he needs help in understanding its beauty.

If the view is spectacular, the beach itself is not, at least not to people expecting sand and Frisbees and long soulful walks. Most people would not even recognize it as a beach; it's small and short and rocky, a shingle beach whose sand shows only at low tide. At high tide, as today, the littoral is reduced to a thin skin of stones and pebbles and cobbles only ten or 15 feet wide, uncomfortable for bodies on blankets except if you're a native Mainer who takes things as they come, and it ends in an even thinner line of shore grasses and beach roses fronting the lawns and seasonal houses on the land.

It's hard to imagine on a quiet winter day like today that a hundred years ago Crescent Beach was a popular and bustling place, and not just with Mainers. By the beginning of the 20th century, steamships were bringing Bostonians and New Yorkers to Rockland, thence by stage to Owls Head. From 1906 to 1917 there was even an electric trolley from Rockland (put out of business, of course, by the automobile). Featured right here were a 700-foot pier, a large hotel called the Crescent Beach Inn that stayed in business until 1982, and a restaurant named the Pavilion that could seat 200 for supper. The patrons were clearly not the barons of Bar Harbor, or the sun-splashers of Old Orchard. If one can loll on sand only at low tide, i.e., for an hour or two a day, then other pleasures must be on offer: row-boating, teas, dancing, games, fishing, rock collecting, promenades on the pier, sitting quietly on rocks – simple, socially oriented pleasures that are seldom found on the privatized shores of today's Maine. Most tourists seek more selfish goals, the perfect tan, say, or the best lobster roll on the mid-coast, or just motoring from A to B.

This bit of beach I stand on at the end of Crescent Beach Road is actually town property, the last vestige of a more populist era. It's a tiny boat landing surrounded by cottages, with official parking spaces for only half a dozen cars, although in summer, especially at low tide, the Chevys and Fords of the locals line the road for a quarter mile, almost all the way back to South Shore Drive. As I look up and down the shore at the row of houses fronting the beach, I wonder how their owners deal with the scores of sun-seekers. Oceanfront property rights in Maine include ownership of the shore all the way down to the low-tide mark, so is there a town ordinance permitting public use of these pebbles and this sand? Or, in the Maine way, is it just an informal arrangement?

I'm most worried about the rights accruing to the monstrous house right next to the landing, since it's brand-new or massively renovated, and separated from the parking spaces by a fence and shrubs only six or seven feet high: how do those poor nabobs its owners (recently landed from the alien world of Weston, Massachusetts, I discover from tax rolls) deal with the great unwashed chewing chips and snarfing Cokes smack in the middle of their picture-window, oriel-window, turret-window views? Is that why it's for sale? Did someone's dream of Maine turn ugly? I imagine the locals gawking and laughing behind their hands: "They'll never get $1.7 million for it – bastards."

If there is controversy or confrontation on these beaches, I haven't heard about it. In Kennebunkport farther south, the abutters on Goose Rocks Beach sued in court to restrict access to the shore, but lost. From the sublime (Goose Rocks is two dramatic miles of perfect sand) to the ridiculous: a lawsuit is being brought here in Owls Head about a few feet of road. A New York couple on Cooper's Beach Road apparently doesn't like the fact that the town has an easement allowing people to WALK ON THEIR ROAD and possibly steal for a moment their view of Rockland Harbor. Dastardly! Walkers must be very dangerous people. I myself walked there recently and didn't realize I was so larcenous, and so in danger of receiving a missile, or perhaps only a yell. Yet I'm sure our New Yorkers have reason for their suit. Perhaps someone seeking enlightenment on the shore actually trespassed on their lawn and bent a blade of grass.

The town is vigorously defending its easement. Its legal fund is over $50,000. Sending a message perhaps?

If I'm confronted on private property while walking, my standard line will be: "Hi, I'm Jim. I live just down Ash Point Drive and I'm doing a little project of walking all the roads of Owls Head. I hope I haven't bothered you." There's only been one confrontation so far. Seeing a barn that I've passed a hundred times before, I walked down its driveway mostly just to say I did it, or maybe to borrow its view of the bay for a second. Naturally, as I was exiting the driveway, a car pulled up beside me and the driver asked, "Can I help you?"

"Ah, I don't think so," I said.

"You were trespassing on my property," he said.

My rehearsed lines failed. "Oh, sorry, I was just walking….I live up Ash Point, Little Island Lane, you know where that is? I walk down here almost every day…sorry."

He was very calm. "It's just I've had some trouble with my neighbors down there," he said, waving his arm at the big houses on the shore. "They don't like my little trailer, think it's inappropriate."

We had a nice conversation after that, introducing ourselves. He's lived in Maine nearly his whole life, and at present was living in his trailer and helping his brother build a house across the road. "They're yapping on about that too," he said. "They think it's ugly. Of course it's beautiful."

I realized later that his last name was the same as one of the roads off North Shore Drive, a prominent name here of long-standing, a road now mostly taken over by people from away. Maybe his rich brother lives there, while he is stuck in the trailer in the shade of the barn. Maybe he's the family black sheep. Maybe…. I'd enjoy meeting him again and finding out. His response to me was gracious on many levels: he obviously detests the gall of his neighbors but perhaps not the neighbors themselves and apparently didn't include me among them.

But if he only knew…perhaps I'm just as guilty as those idiots on the shore so concerned about their property values. In my blog I have criticized that very house John and his brother are building, mostly because they first cut down six acres of trees in front of the house, every single one of them except a few birches. Also, sorry, John, the house is ugly. The first-floor walls are made of rough windowless concrete and seem to serve only to boost the house to a view of the sea (now that the trees are gone). The windows on the two upper stories are pushed out to the corners of the house as if they were wall-eyed. The house rises out of the denuded lot like a prison tower. If you are going to put up a house, at least make it fit the landscape. And leave as many of the trees as you can.

Would I dare to say this if I met John again? Probably not. No wonder Mainers sometimes complain about people like me. We're neither fish nor fowl.

And when I think hard enough about it, I wonder at my own view of beauty. Who is to say that what I see as beautiful is actually so, that what I think should be preserved is so deserving? A house that I dislike may be another man's castle, refuge, paragon of perfect function. Where I laud the pristine, protected summit of Bald Mountain in Camden, others will praise the imposing houses on the top of Dodge Mountain in Rockland. Class division in America doesn't only have to do with money.

Native Mainers may resent being told that people from away are saving the views, the fish, the eagles, the blameless islands from development, that we're saving Maine from itself. Yet human history is undeniably a story of mass consumption and destruction. Here in New England the white pine, the wolf, the cod bear a witness nearly gone. The tragedy of the commons is real, and governments and do-gooders occupy the uncomfortable position of deciding what's right for others, possibly even for the majority of others, on issues the others don't care about. Most people, I suspect, don't care much about conservation. But I remain convinced that the beauty of land and sea is intimately tied to our need for clean air and native species and a pure supply of food. Beauty is gene-deep, and we pave it over at our peril. And so I must try to persuade as many as possible of the salvational power of nature, not millions or even hundreds perhaps, but if just one person through my words were moved to preserve a hillside, set up a trust for the land, live more simply, play hooky, put down the smart phone, look at a goldfinch, I'd hope to be satisfied.

****

But some days hope is not much more than a shuttlecock with feathers. The best use of the land is a thorny subject. Living in beauty cures very little poverty. I walk back up Crescent Beach Road, bothered by an unwelcome, unusual uneasiness of place, by the incongruities of living here. Shores such as these have been batted about, exploited, carved up into little bits of paradise. I'm one of the carvers.

It doesn't help today that the scenery away from the shore is not inspiring. One side of Crescent Beach Road consists of scrub bordered by swamp, the other side a straggly line of small ranch houses. Two of the houses in particular, side by side, catch my eye. One is typically rural: no ornamentation, old vinyl siding, weedy lawn, falling-down shed in back. A clothesline is strung directly across the picture window in front, as if the owners didn't care that their view of grass or snow would sometimes be interrupted by drying underwear. The other ranch is cute-ified: cedar shakes on the walls stained brown, a shed that matches, rock walls, a quaint roped walkway, an ancient graying dory festively parked in the yard with a Christmas tree as pilot, and a fancy sign near the door that says "Wine Down."

I suspect that only a native Mainer would understand the contrast between these two, or possibly his not noticing any particular contrast *is* his understanding. All I can be is supercilious. Furthermore, for all I know or could know, these neighbors are the best of friends. I certainly would not qualify for inclusion in their circle. Exclusion, maybe.

At the end of the road, I think about walking a bit farther east on South Shore Drive to Holiday Beach. It's a lovely area that my wife and I have driven and walked around many times, attracted by what seems to be more of a community, one that has some pride of place. Holiday Beach never got the tourist attention that Crescent Beach did, probably because there's no sand there at all. It developed later, at a time when people wanted something more than a cottage but not yet a mansion. I imagine this as an enclave of Mainers and flatlanders alike, of those who successfully made it through the Depression and the war and the 50s, who worked hard for the right to build a nice place on or near the water. We haven't seen any knock-downs here, or massive renovations. People seem to have kept some perspective on life.

That's more than I can say for my own generation, which after such a promising start in the 60s may have lost its bearings. We became too ambitious, we've worked too hard and so we need to get completely away, in a big house, on a big lot, comforts always close to hand, devices in every room and every pocket that bring the world in and keep it away simultaneously – and those needs have become rights. Worse, for many people such a getaway needs to be in a "famous" place, a Miami Beach, not a Holiday Beach. We need to be seen and noticed, yet able to retreat to splendid, fenced-in, all-consuming isolation. We've poisoned the world, but to keep up our immunities, we need its glances of envy and lances of drugs.

Uncertain, unbalanced, I stand on South Shore Drive as if poised between two worlds. "Nature" is not rescuing me today. Those pretty bushes that I see in a flourish at the end of a driveway were bought at a nursery and unceremoniously planted; they still have price tags on them. The woods of the interior of Owls Head Peninsula seem off-limits and forbidding and winter-weary. The tidal inlets are brackish and green with scum. Cans, envelopes, butts, plastic bags litter the ditches of South Shore Drive. I can't help but think that the beach colonies are aptly characterized. They represent a colonial attitude – patronizing, ambitious, isolating. We come to pray at the water's edge not for enlightenment but for better cell phone service.

South Shore

I decide to forego Holiday Beach and head for home. That's when it hits me. It's not just the beaches and their obvious symbolism that are getting me down. It's what I saw earlier as I walked up South Shore Drive to Crescent Beach, three ordinary scenes that I now realize I actively ignored, that I held in subconscious abeyance, unwilling to think about the discomfort they aroused. The ordinary Maine way of life: it does not yet come naturally. I observe more than participate. What people do is mysterious and challenging. I might even be a little afraid of them, unwilling to invest. That's why I need the shield of a notebook. That's how we concentrate, those of us so easily put off by people. We need a re-visitation, by eye, by word, or by memory, to make sense of a place. Since I forgot my notebook today, I couldn't put pictures into words and store them away for later. I need to re-visit the scenes of discontent, concentrating this time.

I walk back along South Shore Drive. The first image I visit again is a well-maintained house, with a large barn next to it. The barn is slightly dilapidated, with fading paint and a closed-up look. The sign on it, also faded, says Tidal Cove Farm. What a powerful metaphor the saltwater farm is. It conjures up a rich life of soil and sea, an indescribable bounty to be gained on all sides. Imagine the pleasure of forest and field and shore and surf and deep dark waters, all yours and so overwhelming that most emphatically it's not yours at all. Corn and tomatoes and cod, ferns and kelp and trees, deer and goat and gull and cow and eagle all live and grow in the same place. I think – naturally – of E.B. White. How blessed one man could be. How content. How devastating and inspiring his world of neighbors and chickens and heart-rending essays is to cowards like me, making all other lives seem flighty and insubstantial, including mine. But it's a lost world. There are so few such farms, and people, left. They are gone to development, abandoned to scrub forest, caught in ambition.

Tidal Cove Farm looks inhabited but no longer by a farmer/fisherman. Is there a sadder sight than a noble barn used like a suburban garage?

The second item in my litany is a sound first, sight second. A throaty engine roar comes from a lobster boat in a yard, propped up high on supports. Like an iceberg the boat is bigger under the waterline than one would expect, especially a landlubber like me. To get to the deck, the owner has placed a ladder against the boat; I see him descending it as I walk past. I should wave, at least; even better, I should stop to talk to him. I could remark on how odd it is to see an engine running up in the air. I could ask him why. I could ask when he will string his traps again, and how many he has, and how's the fishing going to be this year. I especially want to ask about the name of his boat, Rough Rider III, which implies the prior existence of I and II, perhaps in the same, long-standing family of fishermen. A generation in boat time, I think, is likely to be much longer than in human time. How long has your family lived here? Will your children continue on?

He would be patient with me, I know, in the tolerant Maine way. I probably could learn more in an hour from such a man than a hundred hours of walking would yield. But I don't. The from-away disease strikes again. I walk on by.

Then there's the third image – and maybe I've been uneasy all morning because although the first two are bad enough, this is the one that's so emblematic. On the corner of South Shore Drive and Cripple Creek Lane sits a small house. In the New England way, a structure is attached to it, larger than a shed but smaller than a barn. Its windowless wall faces the road and a mural is painted on it in bright colors. The scene is a cove, perhaps the same one just beyond the shore, with fishing boats and islands and whitecaps and birds. Both the perspective and the rage are primitive.

The blue of the ocean is exceptionally vivid, like a nightmare. A fisherman's bust dominates the sky (or should I say heavens?), the wooden spokes of a ship's wheel framing his sagging bearded face and yellow sou-wester like a halo. On the peak of the roofline above perches a life-sized, wooden replica of a bald eagle. The banner just below reads, in large elegant script spanning the whole wall, "Endangered Species."

I walk as slowly as I can, trying to take it all in, and even consider stopping and gaping until a man drives up in a pick-up, gets out, and heads into the house.

This man I'm not at all tempted to talk to, at least not on his own property, not with his grievances looming so openly. It hardly matters what in the painting that he means to call endangered – the lobster boats, the fisherman, the eagle, the calm and scenic cove ringed neither with big houses nor yachts, himself. What could I possibly say to him? My words would melt away under the righteous heat of his history. I'm part of the problem. I have nothing to offer but my sympathy.

His message is crudely and forcefully put: the lack of working waterfront is an insidious problem for Maine. Its image depends on it. Its industries of fishing and boat-building and sailing require it. Yet only 25 of the 5,000 miles of Maine waterfront are available to the marine industries. The huge majority of the rest is privately owned by people like me, from away, or retired, or both, with a few bits and pieces here and there permanently conserved by government or trusts, like museum exhibits.

Much of this change from wilderness to semi-suburbia happened in our artist's lifetime, I suspect. As a boy in a dory he might have seen only a scattering of private development, in the usual places of town and beach. But now the whole coast is dotted with houses and garages and pleasure-boat docks, and if he still goes to sea, what does he think of the disparities? Hardly any place anymore to put in for a picnic, watch osprey fish, run in some contraband, dig clams or harvest periwinkles, take your girlfriend for a snuggle on an island. That there are still a few places to do these things is also largely due to the flatlanders, those who work in land trusts or government departments of conservation. How would it feel to be a native Mainer, to be assaulted and beholden at once?

But then I look past the mural and see the actual cove, and I walk a little farther to where I can see the sweep of open ocean, and I walk a little farther still into a copse, trespassing, I'm sure, but I'm desperate to feel the solace of trees. A beach of rocks and leaning spruce and rockweed, the forever pull and push of tides, screeching gulls, that's what I need, and I stand for a while in a place without time before heading home.

By the time I'm back to Little Island Lane, I've recovered somewhat. Fresh air and fast walking cure much, even along a well-travelled road. Re-visiting one's assumptions is cleansing. There's a divide among people, and that's regrettable, it's more than regrettable, it's tragic, and we can only hope by individual action to heal it. But yet, in spite of individual need and extenuating circumstances – the tragedy of the personal, if you will – to me it's clear enough that the impulse to consume is destroying beauty and humanity. Have you seen the human blobs in the movie WALL-E? I hope that endangered species of all sorts appreciate the meddling.

And when I get home and write some notes, my faith is restored. Having such a beautiful place to walk in, write in, live in, and even lunch in (with that glorious view of the bay) is a great privilege. I will not underestimate the worth of my sympathy and my attitudes and my words. I too can make a statement of the things I love. Perhaps I can't paint or fish or claim roots on a saltwater farm. Perhaps I have trouble talking to the people who do. But I can try to persuade others to use their talents and their money for the good of the land, and I can write down my own inspiration from trees and tides.

Why do I write about nature? I feel a quadruple whammy, an emotional and spiritual blitz. For example, here's a natural scene that I look forward to at the end of the day, simply this: the sun setting behind the house and the woods, the pointed firs on the shore mostly in shadow, yet for a few minutes their tips blaze with sunlight, and every once in a while, maybe tonight, an American goldfinch will sit on the crown to preen and bask and sing in the last of the light.

So, first: what an incredible gift just to watch and listen to hope made feathered.

Second: when the goldfinch flies away, I will think about what I've just experienced, what it means, if anything, the tininess of bird (and man) against the immensity of sky and water, the cheerfulness and playfulness and sociability of these little marvels, the blessings of free time and walking and exploring in this place. Words and phrases very quickly start to replace the pictures and to roll around in head and heart, wonderfully entangled.

Third: Eventually I will get those words to stop and hold, to connect to each other and to ideas of history and culture, and to inspire emotions all over again, for me and for others.

Last: This is the best way I know to approximate the comfort and the ecstasy of what others call the religious experience, and – what amounts to the same thing – to overcome one's incessant concern with self and the mean stabs of despond and despair. Nature is a kind of perpetual resurrection. Love does this also, and often art and music, but I find it difficult to write about them, as if Mozart and Vermeer and my family's hugs were somehow other-worldly. I can't even try to re-visit them in words. I'll have to get to heaven on the verbs of the goldfinch.

This is how all of us, writer and reader and consumer and dreamer, working together as purely as we can, will undo the habits of our lifetime.

Islands and Points

As far as I can tell, the islands lying off the coast of Owls Head exhibit none of the eccentricity for which many other Maine islands are or have been famous. They are not populated by the crazy, the criminal, the rich, the recalcitrant, the artistic, the asocial. None hosts splendid isolators like Jamie Wyeth in his lighthouse on Southern Island, none is overrun with day-trippers and paint-daubers the way Monhegan is. We have no magnificent Mt. Desert to attract presidents on vacation and the sour cream of New York society. If it's not a contradiction in terms, our eight are ordinary islands. Although I shouldn't really say so – I've not set foot on any of them for relief from mainland mania.

Among coastal towns, Owls Head is hardly unique in possessing islands. Maine has thousands of them, created by dying glaciers which, at the end of the last ice age, scoured the earth like talons as they retreated and melted. Sea levels rose. Valleys became bays, mountains became islands. Little Island in our cove was a knoll, I'm sure, Monroe beyond it a hill. Maine's drowned coast owes its beauty to chaos and change.

Perhaps that's why the islands, for the last four hundred years, have attracted the full range of European eccentricity. An island is a frangible place, and ownership, that European preoccupation, comes and goes like the tides. Today some of Maine's islands are owned singly, crowned by a mansion; some are basically suburbs of Portland split up into subdivisions. Some owners open their fields to sheep and their shores to kayakers as if they were channeling inner Micmacs. Land trusts have preserved a large number of the islands, especially those close to land and land grabbers, but many more are uninhabited, or long deserted by fishermen, farmers, granite quarriers from Italy, post-industrial romantics. And many are owned by no town, no county, no tax-paying person at all. They are unorganized, beholden only to the State of Maine.

In the 1970s the state made an attempt to bring order to this municipal chaos off its coast, namely, to establish ownership and provenance. The Maine Coast Island Registry therefore lists 3,166 islands for which some kind of deed could be traced, from the very large (Mt. Desert, otherwise known as Acadia) to the smallest of ledges (Shag Rock, my current favorite name) barely above water at high tide. The Registry has not been updated, which accounts in part for the wild array of estimates since then of the actual number of islands, in some cases claiming up to 5,000. If I could hike the perimeters of all of them, adding up the mileage as I go, it would be like walking across the country to the Pacific.

Walking is a bit of an obsession for me, and I *have* walked on islands in other, more famous parts of the state, 16 of them in fact: six reached by car via causeway (Beals, Great Wass, Mt. Desert, Deer, Sears, Rackliff); three by car via bridge (Little Deer, Orrs, Bailey); one by car via ferry (Isleboro); three by foot via ferry (Swans, Vinalhaven, Monhegan); two by foot via sand bar (Barred, Fox), and one by foot via causeway (Clark). Each visit is an etching in memory, a walk out of time and into place, never to be forgotten. Yet perhaps it's curious that I haven't done more. There's the fabled pair of Matinicus and Ragged, for example, the farthest of inhabited islands offshore and limned forever in the novels of Elisabeth Ogilvie, or the romantic-sounding Cranberries and Porcupines, or the tourist-heavy islands of Casco Bay near Portland, or even the archipelago in the Muscle Ridge Channel that I see shimmering off the coast of Owls Head at Ash Point. I'm in love with the state. So why not fully experience its most prominent symbol of fantasy, in a kayak, for example, or a windjammer, or just rent a boat and explore, especially when experience till now – seeing the magnificent cliffs and cathedral pines of Monhegan, the wipe-the-drool-off-your-chin viewing of Isleboro's mansions and coves, my wife's and my falling in love with each other and with Maine on Deer Isle – has been so inspiring?

Mostly I stop well short, still on the shore, daydreaming and gazing out to sea. It's as if an island is a fantasy too far. Take one serious trip to Isle au Haut, for example, with its five dozen year-round inhabitants and heights of land and stunning isolation – not just a day trip by ferry, mind you, but a real commitment to camp for a week, for the only inn closed last year – or an extended sail to some of the nearly 200 sites on the Maine Island Trail, and who knows what barely suppressed desires will emerge? My wife and I spent a few days on Monhegan, but that was different, that was a pilgrimage that every Mainer wannabe needs to take, and does, judging by the number of people on the ferry. Even there the desire to escape the world was strong. Any land with four sides of ocean would ensure it. I'm afraid I'd never leave.

Islands can be viewed on most of my walks, but I do most of my serious drooling on Ash Point or Lucia Beach, walking on the Muscle Ridge islands in the imagination, if you will. I'm standing on Ash Point on this cold February day, looking out to sea. The chain of islands in view is not within the borders of Owls Head. It is separate, just to the south and east of the imaginary line in the water, privately owned, almost entirely undeveloped. Some maps call them the Mussel Ridge, apparently after the local blue mollusk, but those cartographers must have been de-poeticized. "Muscle" is the better word, and the deeper root for mussel besides, for the islands look very much like flesh flexed on an arm or a back, bulging from the surface, and on a bright clear day like today, they seem to ride slightly above the water, like Viking longboats.

The channel between them and the mainland is a shortcut for ships going to and from Rockland, and a dangerous one, for although the channel on the southern end is three or four miles wide, it narrows to a few hundred yards in Owls Head Bay, and in years past the elegant three-masters, the pirates, and the groaning lime schooners and granite barges sometimes paid dearly for the hours potentially saved by taking this route – not to mention the danger of the incessant fogs between the warning horns of Whitehead Light and Owls Head Light. Not much problem these days: electronic devices that map depth and seabed contours and GPS coordinates make travel by water boringly safe. And kayakers and day sailors buckle little swash.

In the 19th century a dozen families lived on the Muscle Ridge, fishing mostly, and tolerating a brief flurry of miners blasting granite for the government buildings of Washington. At the north end of the archipelago, Fisherman Island lies bare, with nothing rising vertically but a couple of trees and a small house. I can view it from my deck, and the sight is especially powerful in times of longing and regret. This is the one I imagine living on, and the idea is attractive and painful. It reminds me of the west coast of Ireland, all rock and gorse, a beauty so stark that it hurts to understand trying to live there. Yet the isolation must be magnificent: the endless conversation between water and rock, a way to offer your soul to something both simple and immense, a life stripped to the elements. And those elements define the paradox. The very body that blazes with purity needs carbon and hydrogen and oxygen and their complexities to combust. It needs food, water and possibly even other people. Kelp and periwinkles and the rain and passing kayakers are not enough – not enough to suspire, not enough to blaze. Ergo, the trials and travails of civilization, and Fisherman Island's abandonment to the birds. A sailor friend told me that its owner makes only the occasional visit, in summer.

Those old Mainers who lived in places like this were self-sufficient, more or less. They never confused independence with selfishness, as so many people do today, and that's the attraction of islands: the understanding that the sea transcends differences between friend and rival.

Only fifteen of the thousands of Maine's islands are inhabited year-round. The true islander stays for the winter. He needs only a few people, maybe just one other, maybe none. A caretaker, a postmaster, a lobsterman, a school teacher, he writes in his off hours, or knits, reads of course, walks the shore to see what the tide brought in, watches and waits for a storm, a beached whale, or an emergency for which he can help. On the coldest day of the year, the sea smoke drifts like fog and the rocks are carapaced in ice and the sun stays so low he can safely view its brilliance all day. Winter on the Maine coast, with its ever-green of spruce and its often-blue of water and sky, carries summer within it, painfully and hopefully so, and its sufferers learn to shed time. They make do with what they have for as long as they can.

For the pressure to leave has always been great. Jobs are at a premium. Luxuries enjoyed once a year on the mainland become necessities. Every medical ailment needs a specialist. And now in the press of the 21st century, islands like those of the Muscle Ridge are beautifully, ironically deserted: the very people who most symbolize the spirit and independence of Maine are gone. Fishermen have big motors now and they don't need to live three miles offshore to gain advantage; rich people want cable and croissants; regular people need something to do; only a few artists are as well-off as Jamie Wyeth; sick people need regular prescriptions for their bad cholesterol and high anxiety; and weasly romantics such as me think that just to see an island is enough to be rejuvenated.

I'm convinced there's something physiologic going on. Eye stimulates brain stimulates deep-seated need for connection. Neurons are primitive, almost universal in animals. Humans just have a lot more of them than, say, a wolf, and so by memory or will we can suppress the wildness. But it's still there, growling, basking, protecting young, territorial. I suppose that my feeling about islands is the same as my feeling about the great north woods – tangible proof that the unindustrialized life can still be had even if I won't desert civilization and take it.

Islands and Points

****

When I looked out at these islands in the past, they were deserted (according to the US Census of 2000) in reality if not in my synapses. The Muscle Ridge Shoals Township, its official name according to the State of Maine to which it looks for government, counted no residents. Yet in 2010 the census showed a population of six. What's going on? Did the lighthouse on Two Bush Island suddenly forsake automation and engage a family of keepers? Are hippies dropping out again? Whatever the case, it's a small but cheering trend, and one not limited to this township.

All across Maine these unorganized places, comprising half the state's land in fact, are growing faster than the organized half. We've experienced the worst of the 19th century – its industrialization – for a long time now. Are we now going back to experience the best, its romanticism? Whoever those people are that now call Muscle Ridge home, they're showing us that just off-shore, just out of reach, it's possible to dispense with phones, fences, and 401(k)s, where "they" can't get you if you don't want to be gotten.

The realist in me says to make nothing of this trend. After all, there are only 9,000 people living year-round in all of the Unorganized Territories (averaging 2 people per square mile!), and that "fast" growth of a few hundred more? That represents about 10 minutes of new births in India.

The romantic in me loves it.

****

What I claim is a kind of healing imagination when I look at islands may in fact just be laziness. I haven't set foot on any of the eight islands within the town of Owls Head, all within easy reach.

86

I can see three of them from my deck. Monroe lies to the northeast, opposite Owls Head Harbor and maybe a half-mile offshore. It is owned (and conserved) by a family active in the land trust I volunteer for, the present owners of the former Owls Head Inn on the harbor, and it would be easy to get permission to walk its 200 high wooded acres. Sheep Island to its south would be more difficult, since (apparently) rocks and ledges and shoals surround it and make it problematic to land on and therefore inhabit. But heavens, there's the dot of Little Island right in our cove, just a couple of hundred yards from shore, accessible by sand bar several times a year at extreme low tides and I haven't ever tried.

Being closer to shore than the Muscle Ridge archipelago is, the islands of Owls Head have had a brush with development. The terms of Monroe's easement allow the owner to maintain one seasonal house. Sheep Island, formerly known as Crockett's, a prominent name on my own section of shore, is owned by people from Connecticut and is completely undeveloped now, but at one time participated in the long tradition of islands used for summer grazing (there are more than 20 islands named Sheep in Maine). Just on the other side of Sheep, invisible to me, is a tiny ledge that illustrates perfectly the difficulty of fantasy: it is not listed in the Registry, it is named on no maps I've seen except one, where it is called Carter's Nubble. (I hope Mr. Carter's longing was real even if his bump is barely so.) Just off the lighthouse state park lies Shag Rock, probably named after a species of cormorant – it's not big enough to entertain other meanings of the word. In 2011 Maine Coast Heritage Trust purchased Ash Island off Ash Point, from an owner who was very happy, for a million dollars, to give up her development rights to build a hotel and subdivisions. (The island, now wooded, looks as it must have for millennia – but as recently as 1953 it was completely clear-cut, like much of the whole town.) Someone from Massachusetts owns Spaulding Island off Dyer Point, with a seasonal camp there, and the artist's-dream islands of Treasure (with shack) and Emery (without), each of them specks of flat ledge and pointed firs lying off Crescent Beach just waiting to be painted, are kept that way by couples from Crescent Beach and Connecticut, respectively.

I will trespass on none of these. I might never visit them, much less revisit them. That's just as well, for true Maine islands (those inaccessible by car, I mean) are for men richer or braver or weirder than me, and especially for the kind of person who really understands, and is not driven mad by, the ultimate sense of place. People who don't understand think they'll leave their unhappiness on the ferry.

So let these islands remain pure in mind, something to read about in Elisabeth Ogilvie, a way of life still vibrant less than a century ago, something to dream on. Of island living Ogilvie wrote as well as anyone: of the beauty, the peace, the comradeship; of the dangerous storms, the deprivation, the petty and not-so-petty disputes; of one family rooted in place for generations; and of these emotions I can understand embarrassingly little. Trying to understand my one side of limitless ocean is quite enough.

So to the islands let's add a side or two of land....

****

An acquaintance once said, at the start of our first lengthy conversation when I mentioned I lived in Owls Head, "I suppose you live out on a rocky point." She was only half-joking. She herself lives in a big house in Camden and perhaps thinks those in her world are thus divided. She doesn't include islanders, and I understand the distinction. Civilized people don't live on islands. Islanders are either too rough or too smooth. But in the social hierarchy, people who own rocky points are more than acceptable, perhaps even at the top.

Ordinary Mainers no longer live on rocky points. The points have long been taken, mostly for isolation. The ultimate dream for getting away places one in a house nearly, but not quite, surrounded by water, for one needs to drive and isolation must not come at a price. The plumber and the caterer and the chimney sweep and the gardener can be there in a sec. The point of a point is to control human incursions, with rocky, un-breachable shores on three sides, and a gate or a formidably snaking driveway on the fourth. Natural incursions don't seem to bother those who live on the shore. They can easily evacuate in a southeaster, then repair and rebuild as necessary.

At least I can say I've walked all of Owls Head's points. Some are true little peninsulas, like Crockett's or Ginn or Dodge, each with a large house at its end, and their access roads might as well have gates across them (although they don't), for the feeling of trespass is extreme. The other five named points on the maps – Otter, Ash, Birch, Battery, Dyer – are more like wedges into the sea, with two sides of water, and they tend to be either a little more democratic, subdivided for a few wealthy people, or a lot more democratic, preserved for the public.

The point I view every day, looking northeast, is Ginn. It is the middle promontory of a series of alternating projections of land into water – in the foreground, Little Island pointing northwest, then Ginn pointing southeast, and in the background the end of Monroe pointing northwest again – zigzagging the eye in a surfeit of desire. In the far distance, on a clear day, I can make out Islesboro – one last zig at the north end of Penobscot Bay. Ginn lies there like a perfect vision of Middle Earth, for there is a house on the peninsula, a snug-looking one with big windows facing both east and west, perfect possessor of sunrise and sunset, isolation and accessibility. And of course at the very end, where the ledge and rockweed begin, a lone pointed fir grows and even leans a provocative few degrees towards the water.

Ideal, right? Not quite. When my wife and I walk there one day, after some years of lustful eyeballing, the reality is different. Not quite romantic loneliness, for there are two more houses on the point, hidden from our usual view by trees, crowding up very close in fact to The House, and there's an expanse of tarred driveway and old vehicles and junk leading to what we thought was nirvana, and we turn back as if expecting a large German shepherd watchdog to chase our fantasies away. It's like the protected easement of Monroe Island, so idyllic-looking from the comfort of a sofa, yet which my friend tells me is criss-crossed with ATV trails and infested with ticks from its over-population of deer.

So the ideal place for people like me to visit and revisit is Otter Point, next to the state park. It's privately owned, undeveloped, available to the public but not obviously so, a place to tread lightly and reverently. "Leave no trace," exhorts the Maine Island Trail. This means not only that you must not disturb, but that you must leave. You will lose yourself for an hour or a week in a place like this, then revisit. Repeat as necessary. You are no longer merely escaping a frantic life spent elsewhere, on no sides of water. You are healing the ulcers of restlessness. You are away, yet connected. You don't regret the hours in the office, on a plane, in the car, for they brought you here.

Such a refuge is beyond the reach of almost no one. Getting there does require a car, usually, and some deliberate walking out of your comfort zone – state park, neighborhood, office, Twitter – and some time carved out of your busy day. But that's a small price to pay: your gain, when you leave your car and walk on a broken path and sit on a granite ledge, the spruce forest behind, in front the open sea with its islands to dream on, is the calm balance between now and forever.

Roadless

The middle of the Owls Head Peninsula, between the lighthouse and the airport, between North Shore and South Shore Drives, is taken up by nearly 800 acres of nothing much at all. Aside from the driveways serving developments off North Shore Drive, and one or two driveways off South Shore Drive leading to single houses, there are no roads whatsoever, nothing but fields and forests. Naturally I'm dying to explore. But for a long time I assumed that the walking there would be more forbidding than usual, for all of the land seems to be privately owned, with no obvious and safe way in, and a 50% probability of dog or dour owner.

Then I heard about the Walker family. In 2011 the eight Walker siblings, scattered across the country in the usual American way, decided to protect the farm that has been in their family for generations. Their 132 acres in the center of the peninsula stretch from South to North Shore Drives, and they granted the local land trust a conservation easement on almost all of it. I emboldened myself to write to my acquaintance at the land trust and ask if I could meet John Walker, who still lives on the farm, to thank him for his generosity and ask permission to walk his land. "No problem," she replied, "they're wonderful people and since they allow cross-country skiing already…. we appreciate your consideration in asking."

Even more boldly (for me) I now find myself, on a morning in early April, standing on the steps of a white, ramshackle farmhouse, knocking on the door.

Unfortunately, no one is home. With considerable misgiving, I decide to try the walk anyway, without explicit permission, without a clue where I'm going, presumably trespassing, and I park the car on Crescent Beach and walk back up. The Walkers' driveway leads to the back of the house. I suppose I skulk a little in passing by, worried about a watcher in the window. Yet this walk turns out to be the best one I've had in Owls Head.

A long field stretches out in front of me, emerald green with new grasses. Trees line its borders, just barely leafing out in the yellowish green of spring, and the trees merge into a wood that appears endless. There is nothing else, just hayfield and forest and brilliant blue sky that manages to be both cold and warm at the same time.

For a few hundred yards, I walk along the tractor track at the field's edge. It is lined with junk, almost all of it rusty remnants of discarded wagons, carts, cars, and ATV trailers, like a poor man's Owls Head Transportation Museum. I stop and look back at the house. What appears to be rustic from the front looks poverty-stricken from the back – porch steps tilted, weeds high, and the clapboards aren't even painted, as if there was only enough money to keep up appearances from the road. Bless such a family, obviously strapped for income, yet so generous as to donate an easement that reduced the value of their land by 95%. No cashing out for the greater glory of subdivisions here, ever.

As I walk through the field, I think of land trusts, and bless them also. Some 20% of Maine's 22 million acres are now protected in one way or another by land trusts, wealthy individuals with a conscience (John Malone of cable TV wealth, Roxane Quimby who founded Bert's Bees), state and national parks, and enlightened programs like Land for Maine's Future and the Maine Farmland Trust trying to survive the onslaught from the state's current Tea Party administration. Huge tracts of the Great North Woods are protected, exquisite coastal vistas are saved, and the movement has kindled a new interest in farming. There are 100 land trusts in Maine alone, promoting not only places "forever wild" but also public use of those places. The range of activities is staggering, and will become even more so as a movement towards more community participation, like a town owning a forest for recreation or sustainable logging, or Somali refugees working an abandoned farm, takes hold. What an antidote to land grabs, greed, obsession with fortune! How better to heed the voices of John Muir and Aldo Leopold! The thrushes and the cattails, even next to an expanding airport, are valuable again. Some day we may even convince our grasping world of their economic value.

This is not to say the danger is past. At 95% Maine has nearly the highest percentage of private land ownership in the country, a blessing when the owners are enlightened, a curse when they are real estate investment trusts concerned only with profit. Inevitably, business must expand. People want to build second homes, or view wilderness from an RV. Families will vacation in tents if the camp has broad-band. Sensible development is still hard to accomplish. But the successes of land trusts, even during the recession, and the education they actively and passively provide, are changing hearts and minds.

I soon lose sight of the Walkers' house, and the disquiet of intruding on someone else's land quickly fades. Open spaces do that for a body. The first field links to another, then another, and another, like emerald drops on a chain. Even if I find no trails in the woods, this is enough, a glorious day in the open, the work of man blending lightly and perfectly with dirt and tree. It's a blank slate: I don't see any wildlife and don't expect to this early in the year, but these edgescapes will draw creatures of all kinds. I wish I could come here every day this summer, cataloging the changes. This is the kind of place where the only intrusive thing that happens, I assume, is periodic mowing of the hay, and of course the footfall of deer and the excavation of vole and the buzz of bee and the sensual turn of the season's wheel.

At the end of the last field I find a trail. It leads seductively into deep woods of tall spruce whose height suggests there's been no logging here for several generations. The trail is level, easy, boggy in places, a perfect place to be away. It's easy to imagine I'm hiking the Great North Woods a hundred miles north. Even this small wood within a couple of miles of road and store and house feels like true wilderness. I stop worrying about any challenge to the day's joy, philosophical or physical.

Well, not quite no challenge, not quite no intrusion. A sign soon offers the antidote to a complete swoon of nature. "To Post Hill," it says, pointing one way, "Back to Walker fields," the other. Its orange color can only mean it's a trail for snowmobiles.

Well, here's a nice dilemma. I can hardly think of something I despise more than such a machine: noisy and dirty and thrilly-speedy, the perfect polluter, the ruination of a quiet winter's day. And the people who ride them might be unspeakable too, except that in effect they've created the bliss I have today: a quiet, clean, slow-minded refuge in which this man finds his own thrills. Bless them also, I guess, except in winter when I'll stay away, speaking no evil. Live and let live is the Maine way.

In fact, I discover that the whole acreage is laced with snowmobile trails, increasing my debt to the machines. *Custodia ex machina.* First, I take the track to Post "Hill." I put the word in quotes because the hill is more like a bump. Indeed, the Maine Atlas shows only one contour line (an 80-foot change in altitude, according to the legend) in this whole area. The fact that it's named suggests some past habitation, but when I leave the path and "climb" up, I see no sign of it, no foundation, no cellar hole, no former field. There must have been no advantage to living here, on this thin poor soil too far from town. Very many years ago Mr. Post must have decamped for Ohio.

This part of the trail ends at North Shore Drive near Dynamite Beach Road, down where the rich people live, if you recall. At the trail head I'm happy to see another sign, not orange, saying something like "All motorized vehicles except snowmobiles in winter are prohibited." It's a good place to advertise the restriction; a small lay-by invites use, and there are no houses around to deter malfeasance. An open trail from a busy road invites all manner of activity. But who put up the sign? Who's prohibiting what? Locals disliking the ATVs of the rich? Summercators hating dirt bikes? Landowner with a love of summer quiet? No matter. I'm grateful for small favors. Someone is monitoring these woods.

I retrace my steps past Post Hill and take the branch pointing back to Walker fields. The land changes a little. I'm now on the south side of the hill, and the woods are sparser, with more young hardwoods and brush and fewer conifers. There's a raspberry patch, and then the ruined foundation of a house appears. Sunlight is stronger here – the land was cleared more recently, then abandoned to skinny alders and birches. There's no evidence of a road, or driveway, and I think immediately of a cabin in the woods, like my family's when I was a teenager, like Thoreau's when he too didn't want to be an adult. We – he and I and similar suburbanites – can get away just a couple of miles from town. With only a minimal amount of remonstrative and apologetic blushing for our cars and his Concord, we all can have the best of both worlds. The only thing missing in this particular haven is water: a cold and rushing stream, a kettle pond, a huge northern lake, a sheltered tidal inlet. Necessary for me, but perhaps not for others.

Was the owner of this place a dreamer or a neurotic? A romantic or a misanthrope?

Beside the crumbly foundation of rocks, the only clues are an un-rusted tin cylinder of uncertain use, and a heap of rusted iron looking like some kind of former vehicle. They suggest nothing of motive or content. I sit for a while on rock steps. Sunlight dapples the moss, the low bushes, the lichen on the rocks. Birch leaves flicker. If I stay long enough, deer will quietly arrive, grouse will pick their way through the grasses. It's the kind of place one treks to, backpacks supplies in to. At one time there may have been bear and moose here. I get the sudden notion that this was a hunter's cabin, where men bonded and escaped from women in rituals I don't understand. Ach, probably not – probably my overheated imagination again, based on no facts at all.

The trail does indeed come out at the Walker fields, and I resign myself to retracing steps and braving the forbidding Walker house again. But then I see a couple of orange ribbons tied to a tree across the way and discover the beginning of a third trail. What an incredible day! More brand-new territory, at least to me. I don't care how many Sno-Cat treads and Timberland boots have scuffed these trails before me. True discovery has nothing to do with ego, everything to do with openness.

This trail goes eastward towards the village. A few minutes in, my unknown guide has posted another sign helpfully pointing to "Store," which means the Owls Head General Store, I assume, for re-supplying the beer and the gorp. For a good half-mile I again walk in complete peace and quiet. A glimmer of understanding arrives: I never before quite understood why local people are often so opposed to land trusts and their preserves and easements, or to state and national parks, but now, experiencing these trails obviously maintained privately, without outside intervention, I can see their point. No land trust steward, no park ranger needed. We take care of our own.

But of course such tactics work only if the pressure to use the land remains low. I don't see anyone else today on the trail, nor on a subsequent day walking with my wife. It's the famous places that need help. If it weren't for tree-huggers like the Eliots and the Rockefellers and the Hancock County Trustees of Public Reservations, Acadia would be Long Island by now. Without the benefaction of Governor Baxter 150 years ago, Katahdin would be Mt. Fuji. So why don't people see that the Great North Woods will eventually be cut down, the shores of the huge lakes mansion-ized, the ponds acidified, the brook trout driven from their streams by warming waters? Why don't we all fiercely embrace the idea of a Maine Woods National Park?

As if in support of my obsessions, it's on this trail that I see my first bit of trash, a faded Budweiser can. Nothing before this, not a Doritos bag, not a tissue, not a condom, not an empty pack of Camels. I must be getting closer to the village.

A branch off this trail leads me to a big modern house and next to it a cemetery, most of whose headstones honor a family named Emery of the 19th century, and most of whose stones are fallen down. There is no road leading in or out anymore. Weeds are taking over, the forest soon to follow. It will become a place of unintentional "green" burials, freed from the egoism of history. The names of the stones will fade, the bones in the coffins will crumble.

More signs of civilization appear – a campfire pit, two more Budweiser cans, a plastic wrapper, a can of Red Bull. What kind of person needs stimulants in the woods? OK, don't answer that. Then there's a series of serious stone boundary markers, tall and sculpted, not just iron pins with little orange flags. Beyond them I see what looks like a farm of birches. Someone seems to be growing them, in clumps of four or five trunks, acres of them, or maybe a landscape painter cleared his land except for these scores of picturesque groupings. Why the attempt to improve on perfection? To me the woods don't need it, nor does land need to be marked like a museum. Art should take what comes.

At last and regretfully, not wanting this walk to end, I come out to something I recognize from a previous walk from the other direction, a brown house set on a huge lawn. The trail seems to stop here. I could just skirt the edge of the lawn to get to the village, but a man is mowing, and I turn right to avoid him. But that result is even worse than presumed trespass. I see a large, black shape moving on a driveway and hear barking that becomes increasingly loud. Turning ignominiously around, I high-tail it back, nearly running. A dog marks his property too.

My idyll has come to an end. Choices are now made for me. I scurry to the edge of that big lawn and wave to the mower. He waves back, friendly, as if I were a local. That's why I wear binoculars around my neck – birdwatchers are probably harmless, even gormless. Appropriately enough, I come out on the road where William Buckminster's former junk yard has gone back to field.

In the interests of time and lunch I walk back along South Shore Drive towards my car. The houses and the paved road take me out of worship, back to analysis. I think about the amount of land in Owls Head that is protected. The Walker farm is the ninth such property: the number of easements now totals four, there's the Paul Merriam Nature Park courtesy of the Transportation Museum, a land trust owns Ash Island, the state operates the two state parks, Owls Head Light and Birch Point Beach, and finally, there's the wildlife management area called Weskeag Marsh that I've yet to explore. Total protected acreage is 14% of the town's land, under the state's average, but if you add in this roadless tract, that percentage nearly doubles. Not bad for a poor and semi-rural place unspectacular in the normal sense.

So I must now add small-lot owners to my list of benefactors. How many millions of acres do they control? They are the most vulnerable to the financial sharks, I know, but maybe represent the next wave of preservation, once we've gotten as much of the stunning and diverse and pristine as we can under contract. An ordinary woods for ordinary people heals like any Acadia.

And I would have known not nearly as much of the beauty in Owls Head, would have experienced only a few of these remarkable places if I hadn't gotten out in the most ordinary of ways and walked these places, revisiting them in person where I had only walked in my mind.

Halfway back to the car I see an old woman toiling up her driveway towards her mailbox. She's using a walker and going very slowly. I bid her good morning.

"Chilly, isn't it," she replies.

"Yes," I say, "it looks warm but really is a little cold when you're out in the wind."

"This is the first time I'm out this winter," she says. "My husband died recently, and now I'm all alone."

"I'm very sorry to hear that," I answer.

She stands still, looking at the past.

"I'm Jim," I say. "I live down Ash Point way."

"I'm Helen." She smiles. "A long way from home."

"Oh, not so bad. I parked the car at Crescent Beach, been walking the snowmobile trails."

"Lovely day for it."

"Beautiful."

"Well, Jim, it was nice to meet you." She carefully moves the walker forward a few inches. "Have a good day."

"You too."

I look at her house as I'm walking away. It's very small, down an incline, in good shape. It looks out at woods in the back, and a sliver of the bay beyond. I hope she can continue to view the woods, to walk up that driveway. She said she was all alone. I hope that means only in the house, I hope there are children nearby, and if there aren't, as is so often the case, I hope that friends and neighbors will watch out for her. If Owls Head is the kind of place where snowmobilers take care of the land.... As if to confirm my hopes, the sign in front of the Owls Head Baptist Church advertises a benefit dinner for the food pantry.

I return to the car and sit quietly for a while, looking out on the water. Today's walk was one of the best not only because it was unexpected, or was new territory for me. It was because I walked on paths made for feet (at least in summer), not roads made for cars. In the middle of nothing, I thought about humans, not lynxes. I thought about community and the community's place in protecting what it loves. In the middle of nature, for once I didn't gripe (much) about people.

It's quite easy to imagine my place in wilderness – the connection to tree and deer is obvious and strong in my heart. It's much harder to know how to live in society. The competition is much more complicated when we've lost the ability to live within our means. Ironically, places that seem to live within their means – small towns like Owls Head, for example – are in some trouble. Owls Head has lost population according to the 2010 census, but I'd bet that the usual story – old people die, young people move away to have their babies – is supplemented by people from away, buying or building houses that are counted only in the tax rolls. Wealth is maintained, but people like me tend not to think very locally. Helen the widow won't figure highly in our week-day charity or our year-end giving. The prospects of fortunate and unfortunate alike are sometimes enhanced, sometimes masked by the beauty of the place.

My own impact on this community has been minuscule. I tell myself I must attend a bean supper at the former grange or a meeting of the Mussel Ridge Historical Society, or invite our Crockett neighbors for tea and their take on local history, or contribute to the food pantry. Inevitably, I postpone, make excuses. Maybe it's fairly common, maybe a lot of people like me like to have things to look forward to on the calendar, a fundraiser, a party, or even a business trip, looking so fresh and inviting on the calendar underneath the pretty picture of Acadia from the Natural Resources Council of Maine, or in the bright colors of Google Calendar. For the need to advance psyche or career is strong. The mere fact of future engagements makes restlessness seemed justified. But then the event comes closer, and the excuses start, or hope springs up that a blizzard, a flu, anything, will intervene to delay or cancel.

Responsible me usually muddles through, however, sometimes even enjoyably, and if the moment of accomplishment doesn't always feel satisfying, at least there's relief when it's over. From this waffling I might exempt an intimate dinner party, but after a few hours even with the best of friends, I get antsy. There's nothing left to talk about. It's time to go. I will love them in retrospect. In modern parlance, "Being sociable is not who I am."

That so great a man as Thoreau apparently thought the same way ("It appears to be a law that you cannot have a deep sympathy with both man and nature.") is some comfort, but misanthropy is Thoreau's dark side. I worry that unease with anyone not wife or daughter is indeed misanthropic. Is hermit just another word for coward? When is selfishness justified, if ever? Taking humans on their own terms is frightening – too much pain and cruelty in those terms. I know I'll never understand the energy and excitement of crowds, and that's OK, but I also worry that Forster's great epigraph "Only connect" and Thoreau's plea for "Contact! Contact!" are sadly beyond my grasp.

Why this agony of people, this ecstasy of eagles? It might have to do with restlessness (I for one find rest more easily with the latter), that one doesn't stay in any one place for very long. The great wide world distracts and attracts. If we do happen to see an eagle, we think about its symbolism, not its essence. We are often unsatisfied with the present job, house, spouse; we yearn to replace them, or at least travel to some place other than the place we are stuck, and if we can't escape in person, we'll do so by screen. If someone builds a road, we will take it.

Only one of the Walkers, for example, kept his deep allegiance to the land, but all of the siblings felt its pull. We don't stay in one place long enough for the land to work its magic and build community. True community is not limited to the rural communities of the past and present. It can also be strong in a barrio, in a suburb. It must be tied to place, however (please, let's not mention virtual communities), for what do people do when society disappoints and fails? What is left then but family and the land? (Please, let's not mention religion.) And when family also turns poisonous?

The poisoning of land is the ultimate insult. That's why I volunteer for a land trust as my own rock of ages. I love my family for I know they won't fail to be good, and I write about a Nature where evil and good are meaningless, hoping to contact, hoping to connect, hoping to justify a life. Mostly fine for now, while I have energy to write and work and love.

But as I get older, I expect horizons to shrink, paths to narrow, roads to shorten, circles to reduce. Time spent in loneliness will increase. Bad habits may solidify. Then will I regret isolation from the people of Owls Head? Are birds and words enough?

I don't know. I try not to look forward (that old Calvinist tendency) too much, to worry about the road ahead, but I'm pretty sure that the end of life is roadless. If so, that makes wandering in place a very good answer. I won't be frightened to find out that my path becomes a circle.

When our neighbor Lydia died, scores of her friends and neighbors and relatives gathered at her house on the shore for her memorial, except her daughter, who had arranged to sail into the cove by boat. The boat – a lobster smack – arrived, and a bugler played Taps from the second-story deck high above the lawn. Another bugler in the boat answered back. The mournful notes echoed round and round. There was a moment of silence. Then her daughter scattered Lydia's ashes in the waves, and at once, as if human actions were insufficient, a brilliant shaft of sunlight pierced the clouds at the moment of release.

There are no roads to Lydia's grave. "Ashes to water, water to life" sounds better to me than "Ashes to ashes, dust to dust." Like Lydia, I'd prefer to live on as an intense memory, however short, than under a cracked headstone.

Helen of South Shore Drive, recent widow, will probably find peace more quietly and conventionally, next to her husband in a plot in the cemetery. Her history will have a road to it, for Owls Head was her long-time home. She'll find comfort with her neighbors. Hermits and transients may find a different solution, a bluer one in the ocean, a greener one on a hillside. Their molecules will be free to roam, and may bump into great-grandfather Albert much more quickly if not contained by a casket. Some of us between homes have not yet booked our body's fate. But whatever our choice of departure, we are fortunate to have experienced a place that lays benedictions on us all.

If maps are the voyeur's substitute for adventure, then I must be a champion of the species, for I have more than enough guides to the bits and bobs of wetlands in the town of Owls Head. Not a real voyeur, of course, sitting in a dark room and drooling over contour lines: however timidly, I'll actually get out and explore these saltwater and freshwater swamps, the last unknown and roadless territory within our little town, at least to me.

Map #1 is the Shoreland Zoning map on the town's website, showing in four colors the restrictions on development for any land partially wet. The saltwater ocean shore of the peninsula shows three of those colors. By far the most prominent is yellow, for Rural Residential, i.e., land can be bought, sold, developed, and taxed with only some relatively minor hassles about setbacks and footprints and leaching fields and the preservation of appearances. But there's also a goodly and satisfying amount of bright green – the whole shores of Monroe and Sheep and Ash and Spaulding Islands, plus several private easements and the two state parks – which color signifies the much more stringent zoning called Resource Protection. Here you can do nothing, not even cut a tree, thank goodness. It's also good to see, or maybe not depending on your interest in money, that the amount of orange, the third color on the coast, is minuscule. That designates commercial zoning, and in Owls Head, we have only the two lobster companies on the harbor, a dot on South Shore Drive near the shore and one on Crescent Beach, use unknown for either, and a worm-like blob representing the air terminal and Budget Car Rental, curling up to one of the swamps near the airport.

Inland, the map shows fewer, but still some, of those places painted bright green. There are the four blotches of protected wetlands playing tic-tac-toe around the two crossed runways – the "mitigation" awarded us and ducks when the airport expanded. A small bog is located at the Head of Bay near Ingraham Hill, too small to tramp. The other bog, however, in the far northwest corner of town is obviously an extension of the large, saltwater Weskeag Marsh in South Thomaston, and will be my destination for this Monday morning in July.

Finally, the map shows one blob of a fourth color – lime green – and it is labeled somewhat less memorably: "Resource Protection for Moderate & High Value Freshwater Wetlands as rated by IF&W 7/14/08." A destination for another day, this bog lies across Route 73 from the airport, in the shadow of the suburban developments on Ingraham's Hill, and extends just slightly over the South Thomaston line. It looks very attractive, a couple of hundred acres at least of promises and unknowns, with birds certainly, perhaps masses of ducks, for why else would Inland Fisheries and Wildlife for the State of Maine protect the area, and indeed draw its own map (Map #2, also on the town website) of the preserve, if not to secure breeding grounds for ducks to be shot elsewhere?

Map #3 gets to the point of today: this one, again from IF&W, shows the entirety of the Weskeag Marsh, formally called the R. Waldo Tyler Wildlife Management Area. It sprawls for hundreds of acres, and just a corner of it pokes into northwest Owls Head. There are no roads and no paths that I can see. It's a least a half-mile hike in, through the bog or over the hills. Maybe I'll try to reach that corner, maybe not.

And, of course, I always have Google Maps, and forever and ever, the *Maine Atlas.*

On the *Atlas* the Weskeag River looks like a squashed, multi-legged salamander, its head the reversing tidal currents under the bridge in South Thomaston, its body the main channel of the river, its limbs and tail the meandering waterways of the marsh. I've driven out of the village center of South Thomaston along Buttermilk Lane, following the river, seeing the marsh from the height of hills and the comfort of the car. This is the way to the town dump and the bottle redemption center, which lie between the marsh and the commercial development on Route 1; I'm well used to seeing the curving beauty of the road end suddenly in something else altogether.

As usual I carry nothing with me but binoculars and a notebook – no maps, no phone with GPS, just an open mind. It's bad enough to be distracted all one's life by paperwork and computer screens. Not here: I'm outside, I'm free and wandering and slightly nervous, growth and decay acrid in the nose and thrilling in the eye.

At the bottom of the last hill, I cross the river and park in the lot facing the marsh. The local land trust has put up information panels describing the marsh and the birds – Weskeag is one of the premier birding places in Maine, especially during migration. The view is simple, a classic salt marsh: winding channels, grasses, woods at the edges. Just one white egret on display but that doesn't really matter. The point is not to add to one's life list of birds; the point is to cleanse one's life by senses and tide.

Recently, the land trust and IF&W constructed a trail nearby that leads to a viewing platform a quarter mile in. The trail is a pleasant one, through mixed woods, away from the marsh, unexceptional except that weirdly, five minutes along, I come upon a pile of large, whitened bones. Must be cattle, I think, but they look collected here and why would someone do that? I can only think it's a subtle reminder that in the past, people found salt marshes extremely fertile places for livestock and agriculture. This woods of young trees perhaps had been a pasture, and the marsh could have been slated for damming and filling – what a nice level meadow for the grazing of cows! Now the woods is a barrier and the marsh is protected and the only farm is an organic one just up the hill, although it is one that not too long ago grazed sheep on the slopes around the marsh. Maybe this ossuary marks a place where an info panel on agriculture will be built.

The trail ends on a deck. Here one looks but doesn't touch; the deck is raised and there's no path to the water. It affords just a taste of the marsh, no need to get wet and into the quagmires, no encouragement to get muddy or explore off trail or even get lost. Rather the opposite. In the distance, I see a couple of white egrets, and some other birds like swallows carving the air, and a sandpiper (or stilt or snipe). I'm no birder but maybe I'll return during migratory season. Yes, a revisit: the promise of returning is as important as the first visit. To find something new in a familiar place is as exciting as seeing the place for the first time, possibly more so. At least to romantics like me.

That must be what migratory birds experience on their impossible journeys. Each stop is a familiar and welcoming one, yet each is also a potential break in a fragile ecological chain. The annual migrations of birds (and human farm workers) might be the only true international experience. If something happens to the Weskeag, for example, or the Rachel Carson marsh in southern Maine, the ecology, the diversity, even the culture of lands both north and south could be affected. Birds protect habitat as well as any photogenic polar bear, and their presence makes a salt marsh a place of connection and protection like no other. For a marsh not only performs hydrologic and chemical services, such as cleaning polluted water, protecting shorelines, preventing floods and recharging aquifers, but it also supports great biodiversity and complex food chains. And its stark and elemental simplicity reminds us of the salt water in our veins.

Compared to the riot of vegetation in the woods I just walked through, the salt marsh is plain – mud flats, spartina grasses, some cattails exploded – and it is ruled by little more than tides and salinity. Its open water looks blue from a distance but is muddy and brown. One gets the feeling that life in and under the water is much richer than above, thriving with mollusks and minnows, worms and bugs, hence the birds.

And now it's time to stop being a tourist, it's time to morph into trespasser. It's "adventure" time – not only no roads where

I'm going but potentially no trails or track – and I'm going to try to get into Owls Head in a most unusual way, from the wedge of the marsh. I take a couple of cracks at it.

I don't remember from the morning's review of the IF&W map where exactly I should be going. First I try the field lying on a hillside directly across Buttermilk Lane on the north side of the river. I hop the ditch, and plow through waist-high weeds, more or less following deer paths and the places of flattened grass where they rest, until I reach the top. There's a fence. I can see the Weskeag Farms vegetable stand, and a tiny pond below, and the coarse towers of Dragon Cement in the distance. No paths present themselves. I won't trespass so boldly as to climb a fence. Strike one.

I walk back to the road, intending to explore the woods that lie closer to the river. As if on command, a duck and seven ducklings file across the road just ahead, perfectly spaced in a line. They really do this – my children would be pleased to know. And in rural Maine, they need no policeman to make way; traffic on Buttermilk is light. I wonder briefly why they didn't just take the culvert under the road to get to the other side, but then realize they must be heading for the fresh water of the pond. Which makes me want to see that pretty little pond, makes me drawn to it like a boy to a treasure chest of frogs and water lilies and fish and ducks. I try to scout its edges. But the vegetation is too dense, bushes and shrubs and full-grown trees, all thriving on the sweet water, which lies unaccountably right next to the road and just a few steps away from the poison of the tidal salt. It's like a bit of Eden in there, lush and fecund. Anything can grow near a pond, especially dreams, but only strong and fallen beings apply for employment in a salt marsh.

I do find a vehicle track, however, and being weak and easy I take it through the woods above the river. This is familiar again, walking among quiet spruce and oak, coming upon a glade and pushing through its profusion of shoulder-high pink flowers, listening for birds, watching for lynx. But soon enough, after a mile or so, I see a cat, an old car, a house just beyond the tree line – and that's the signal to return. On days like this, familiarity with the accomplishments of humans breeds contempt. I'd rather bury my head in a thicket.

On a slightly different trail back, I can see the marsh and the river, but it's down a slope and access looks difficult. This adventurer will continue to look for an easier way, so it's back to Buttermilk Lane, and the bridge over the culvert to the other side of the river, and the more open view east along the narrowing channel of the refuge.

The third attempt: I stop on the bridge, weighing the chances of mud. The channel looks inviting: flats of grass on each side of the muddy tidal flow, lines of shrubs just above the marks of high tide, fields and woods above that. But who knows what muck the flats conceal, and me in my sneaks. Weaseling out, I walk down the road a bit where access is easier, to more former pastures, in fact, and I push up the hill, through weeds, yet again. After some climbing towards the woods, the effort becomes a little embarrassing. I'm avoiding the real issue.

I've pretended that I want to walk into Owls Head from South Thomaston, just to be able to say so, I guess. But I have no idea where the town line starts, and town lines don't really matter when you're trying to be a deer and not a tax payer, and what's the point of such a goal anyway? The point of this day was to explore something completely new to me, a salt marsh, not fall back on the familiar woods and fields, and so far I've just skittered safely above its edges. How can I revisit a marsh, and really see its wonders past the novelty of the new, if I never visit in the first place?

Emboldened, I walk back down the field, crossing a couple of little ravines, one of which obliges by trapping my foot in mud for a moment; negotiating what looks like tractor ruts, into one of which I slip and fall; eventually ending up at marsh's edge only slightly undignified by dirt.

It's low tide. Here on the tidal banks of the brook, the ground under the spartina is relatively firm. The grass whispers against my legs. It is thick and tough and fragile, the only thing growing here, the only plant adaptable, a monoculture in the mud. This is the barrier between water and land, a place whose strength is in its give, built for storms but not, perhaps, for oil spills and certainly not for dredges. What better image is there for tenacious simplicity?

As it turns out, the firmness of the ground means I could have walked a long way upstream along this channel, and possibly even back south into the main marsh, before the tide came in. And now it's too late – next time I'll check on the tidal tables, and have a wonderful and meandering revisit, but this walker needs lunch, and an afternoon to recoup his energy.

Before I go, I stand on the bridge and look back once more towards the river source. I can see a bit of Rockland's industrial park to the east but all the development on Route 1 – that modern swamp – is invisible from here. But it's there, I've shopped at the Lowes that lies on the very headwaters of this marsh; from here, you would never know what grotesqueries lie just a half mile away. In the marsh I close my mind to Route 1. On Route 1 I can't stand to think of the marsh. We divide things so neatly in our minds; such schizophrenia allows us to live with what we've done.

Later in the afternoon, after food and rest, while I re-think my morning, Google tells me what my legs dared not.

It's a different kind of journey, pursuing a thread on Google Maps. It's a kind of vicarious revisiting, showing me what I cannot, or will not, see from the ground. At the very least it's hard to stay romantic in the crude colors and child-like renderings of Map View. Satellite View is better (at least you can turn off the labels), but the hand of man is still obvious. Take the main part of the marsh. Some of its multiple channels, especially those near the road and therefore near houses and people, are perfectly straight. Why? A little searching tells me the marsh suffered a technique called grid-ditching, to provide more flooding and therefore mosquito control. (Unlike other mosquitoes, those of saltwater origin lay eggs on soil, not in standing water, and don't survive frequent immersion.) For a square inch of salt marsh silt is said to contain as many as 20,000 mosquito eggs in season. You appreciate the municipal challenges.

But why this was necessary in sparsely populated rural Maine must be an example of technology begging for an application. Fortunately, the history of mosquito control in marshes – from hand-dug grid-ditches in the 30s to massive applications of pesticides in the 50s to the hydraulic engineering schemes of the present – seems to be one of failure, now that we've mostly stopped the ultimate form of control, draining and paving over the mess. For once, ecosystem health may be winning over individual discomfort.

Where the damage in the main part of the marsh is subtle, what happens to the marsh at its northern end is impossible to ignore.

The Weskeag flows through that culvert under Buttermilk Lane and thereupon changes its name to Marsh Brook (of course a brook is more easily ignored than a river). From there it's mostly one main channel, and as I angle those Google arrows north and east, soon enough ominous icons appear – the factories and warehouses comprising Rockland Industrial Park border directly on the marsh.

Apparently, the brook still flows through marsh when it crosses Thomaston Street just past the factories. It is still Resource Protected for a couple of thousand feet, according to the IF&W map, but it's now terribly narrow and soon enough bumps up against train tracks, and becomes too small to matter. There the blue lines branch, and tangle, and somehow continue through the mess of Route 1– Lowes, McDonald's, Flagship Cinema, car dealers, and the desolate site for a new Walmart recently permitted by the Town of Thomaston – protected no more, obliterated perhaps.

The river's tidal power is long gone. What wetlands still last here must be fresh (is there a word for unfresh wetlands?). How can Google Maps still show thin blue hopeful lines crossing Route 1? Someone's memory? Actual wet spots amidst the concrete and tar? Rivulets diving underground in consternation, coming into view only where the state bans development? Imagine trying to follow such streams to their headwaters – you might end up in the bathroom of an Applebee's, i.e., a journey to the heart of darkness.

Where feet can't or won't go, words must. An eco-trek in prose is like a journey without end. It must boldly go where no one used to be. It recreates the beauty that must have been and makes us grateful for what remains. We must preserve our places of connection. We need the protection of mud flats and grasses and wooded uplands against the tide of development. Every human action, every human goal must be examined. It's that critical.

****

The largest freshwater patch of marsh that I can see on my maps is that bog lying just off Route 73 north of the airport. It's taken me almost a month, now a Tuesday morning in August, to find the right time to explore it, the right time being a bright day empty of land trust meetings, dog walks, clouds, rain, pleasure drives to nowhere, chores, naps, or other responsibilities of the retired.

I park the car in the little lot near the entrance to the Merriam Nature Park so ironically preserved by the Transportation Museum and walk across Route 73. There are hayfields and copses here, and the contrast between them is part of the picturesque charm of New England, the close working relationship between brown and green, tamed and feral, human and wild that one finds in few other places in the country. Once I've walked through the fields, I can see the tell-tale grasses and cattails of wetlands, and a few glints of water. A great blue heron takes flight as I get closer.

Although it's late summer, the driest part of the year, there is the matter of getting wet to consider. My boots are only ankle-high; I'm still at least 50 yards from the standing water and who knows what muck lies between? Tentatively, I try the stand of cattails, which proves to be too wet below – and so the grasses just beyond that clearly will not do at all. I retreat to a drier place and reconnoiter.

Ahead and to the left lies a sloping field, an old pasture perhaps, and a copse next to it that seems to border the standing water. I'll try to approach the swamp there, and I push through the shoulder-high stretch of weeds – varieties of golden rod and aster and impatiens (the pink blossoms of Himalayan balsam are particularly striking) that clog the passage through.

There are no trails, but of course I'm not in any danger. I can see where I'm going even though the weeds are now so high as to tickle my chin. There is no quicksand, probably. It's only slightly squishy underfoot. Snakes would long be departed in my thrashing about (and poisonous snakes have long since left Maine anyway). Mosquitoes bearing West Nile or EEE haven't been found in this part of the state. Ticks can be brushed off, if I remember to check clothes and toes. Even mad dogs are too sensible for marshes. Yet how much of the thrill of bush-whacking is the frisson of danger? (And I don't mean the danger of Lyme Disease.)

Just a hundred or so feet of whacking finds me safe on the hillside, back to familiar smaller waist-high weeds, deer trails and their beds, patches of tiny, sweet blackberries. The copse of trees is quiet as I walk through. I get to within 15 feet of water – a couple of ducks, vegetation dying in the late summer heat – before the squish underfoot threatens to become a splash and I turn back. As often happens, the goal should be just an excuse for the journey.

I retrace my steps all the way back to the edge of the hayfields, and look once more through the binoculars, as if saying goodbye. Two large brown birds are visible in the water, perhaps geese, since they seem both to stand and swim and I don't know if ducks or herons do that. When I'm home, I'll try to identify them in Sibley's, but I'm not really serious about it, not obsessed with genera and lists and naming names, not boasting strong binoculars, not clothed and equipped by L.L.Bean. In all likelihood they will remain "two large brown birds."

I suppose that if I had any regrets in my life, it would be the lack or denial or avoidance of true adventure. For someone who loves nature, I know nothing about white water, tops of real mountains, tropical jungles, trekking map-less. For someone who has travelled to many places in the world, I never took the extra time after a conference or a business retreat to float in the Dead Sea, climb Mt. Fuji, dive in the Great Barrier Reef, ride the pampas, ski the Alps, hike the Scottish Highlands. I guess I like "normal" nature, the beautiful quotidian. I don't need to collect trophies. I like to visit places that I can re-revisit.

And this faint note of apology is okay. I don't really regret too much except for not truly understanding the regional wonders, like the top of Katahdin or the 100-Mile Wilderness Waterway. People, myself included, have caused enough damage by flying about and trekking around and "discovering" the world. We might be more content and more productive by staying local. Besides, adventurers often become, or are certainly followed by, the domesticators. Look at all the synonyms for the word marsh. Swamp, bog, mire, fen, quagmire, slough – think what emotions they arouse, what dangers, discomfort, and pain. These are places to fill in, level, develop, pave over, poison, make into malls.

These are the places that become "Thomaston Commons."

Remember that Walmart about to arise? Thomaston Commons is the faux New England name for the Walmart Supercenter that's going to be built on the headwaters of the Weskeag River. (The existing Walmart in Rockland just a few miles away is merely an ordinary one.) It's an equal opportunity despoiler, paving over freshwater wetlands in asphalt and cement, and at the same time potentially polluting the saltwater wetlands downstream, through the run-off of oils and chemicals accumulating on all those new impervious (yes, that's the technical term) surfaces.

There was some controversy, as follows every new Walmart announcement, and a number of public hearings, but soon enough the authorities of town and state and country duly approved. (It may be hard to grasp, but Maine's Department of Environmental Protection was one of the complicit authorities, and I've found the documentation showing the gory details.) It took Walmart a few years of town meetings, scores of consultants, and piles of paper, but all is well. They will destroy some 100,000 square feet of wetlands, they will pay their mitigation money, and I don't know whether to rejoice or despair. Here's the way conservation really works these days.

In 2008 Maine set up the Maine Natural Resources Conservation Program. Companies proposing to destroy wetlands or other habitat get their permits from the DEP and the U.S. Army Corps of Engineers in the usual way, but now also pay In-Lieu-Fees (nicely abstract wording, don't you think?) into a fund intended to preserve or restore wetlands in other parts of the state. (The fund is administered by the Nature Conservancy, thus with the Corps completing a very strange trinity, especially since DEP is administered as of this writing by a lawyer who previously lobbied for businesses like chemical and oil companies. Sometimes you don't want to know how sausage is made.) In any case, the MNRCP has distributed millions of dollars to conservation projects around the state in just a few years. That volume is both frightening and exciting.

"Mitigation" is the key word. That check for in-lieu-fees from Walmart to DEP, a copy of which I found online, is in the amount of $402,545.78. That's $3.97 per square foot of destroyed wetland (which sounds like a Walmart price: "Attention shoppers, wetlands now on sale in aisle 3"). Who says Walmart isn't environmentally conscious?

Now, all together, let's feel good about 400 grand. And of course I do. I've looked at the list of projects funded by the MNRCP as a result of all these ILFs assessed state-wide over the last few years, and it's wonderful – 23 projects in 2011 alone. The program's governing principle is that "compensation is required to achieve the goal of no net loss of wetland values and functions." Damn them all. I have to agree. If the elected officials of the Town of Thomaston, and by extension its people, flaunt their constitutional rights and want their section of Route 1 to look like other visionary places generating buckets of tax revenue – Homestead, FL and Lynn, MA come to mind – and thereby the Georges River Land Trust, for example, gets $170,000 to help conserve the St. George River's tidal areas, how can I argue? More Walmarts, please!

Setting aside the inanity of building one Walmart so close to another (the one in Rockland will of course be closed), oh, and the embarrassing predation of a huge corporation on a small town's propensity for greed, and the spectacle of yet another cavernous space dealing without conscience in the necessary and the unnecessary alike, not to mention the gobs of climate-changing plastic and the cheapest of sweat-shop imports on sale in that space, this example probably represents a system working well. It's what we can expect in a country dominated by the dollar. Apparently, we must make pacts with the devil to do God's work.

WWTD? Henry David wrote in his great essay "Walking" that "hope and the future for me are not in lawns and cultivated fields, not in towns and cities, but in the impervious and quaking swamps. When, formerly, I have analyzed my partiality for some farm which I had contemplated purchasing, I have frequently found that I was attracted solely by a few square rods of impermeable and unfathomable bog – a natural sink in one corner of it. That was the jewel which dazzled me. I derive more of my subsistence from the swamps which surround my native town than from the cultivated gardens in the village."

Thoreau wouldn't be able to do anything – he'd be gobstruck. Anything he'd say would be ignored anyway, for a man who uses the word "impervious" to describe a swamp, not a parking lot, must be hopelessly out of touch, his world turned on its head.

And so these boggy places, these connections between land and water, may represent one last yin and yang – the difficult marriage between hopeless romantics and savvy bureaucrats. Divorce is no longer an option.

Little Island Lane

Starting in the summer of 1995, my family and I took our refuge from the city in the house on Little Island Lane. Our daughters were sad to leave the summer cottage in central Maine where we would swim and play silly games on inner tubes, but we parents lusted for the coast. Even more than the camp before it, Owls Head was our shelter from careerist America, a calm place to go to and come from in a cycle of long weekends and vacations. The ocean felt much wilder than the lake. There were no water skiers, pontoon boats, jet skis. There were foxes and deer in our woods, often in the yard.

It was not a home, however, not yet. It looked like one, perhaps, with year-round comforts – that is, it wasn't funky and spidery and un-insulated like our North Pond camp, but home was the city, I mean the suburban city, 200 miles and a time- and spirit-shift away. Massachusetts was the place with neighbors and friends, the place that created our responsible and respectable lives, where our grammar was civilized and where we took care with our punctuation.

That was our home because the rewards of the measured suburban argot are well-known. DINK-ing for a few years sets the stage for climbing the corporate ladder, and that produces capital and credit enough for the nice home in the suburbs, children in due course, their protected and challenging schools, the second place in Maine or the Cape, promotions and graduations and trips to Disney World and Provence.

The costs are also well-known. I thought I had them sussed out, that I paid them with eyes wide open. I knew, for example, that businesses (even publishing these days) care mostly for short-term profit; that jobs often inspire not security and satisfaction but a base passion for money either for itself or for what freedoms and distractions from the job it can buy; that one's treasury is abstract and tenuous, friable, merely some retirement projections on a screen; that certain amounts of gastro-esophageal reflux and insomnia are acquired and borne; that children of privilege may develop the problems of privilege; and that for the great majority of people, including me, happiness in suburbia did not extend very far outside family and friends and safety. All these costs I was willing to bear.

The costs for us, thank God, did not include the real horrors of the world, the poverty, disease, and despair of much of humankind. Those were far from our way of life, to be dealt with if necessary in the stereo of NPR or the frisson of the Globe, or by a separate construct of the mind and some vague faith in government and insurance and luck. However, upon retirement in 2008, having taken care of the needs of the body, I may have been wrong about the life of the mind. What brain cells did I lose in endless calculations of future net worth? What creativity was stifled in the 7-to-5 weekday battle, the debilitating business travel? What restlessness ensued from the habits of 24-hour Internet connection, even in rural Maine, to everything?

John Cheever in his journal said he lived certain days of his life as if he were a man in jail, naked, with the door unlocked, not knowing how to escape. I always thought differently, that the walls and the locks and the uniforms of our daily prisons are real enough, but that retirement would be like busting out of them. What Cheever meant, and I now worry he was right, is that the most frightening thing about prisons may be how they change their inmates, what invisible walls they raise. What if we serve our sentences, shed everything, and still can't leave the cell? The means of escape may be everywhere around us, yet we don't know how to employ them.

One of my means of escape, starting at a very young age, has always been fiction. In the bustle and constrictions of life, as I grew up lonely and accumulated things and provided security for my family, books were like a walk in the prison yard. I clung to them, reading novels, and soon enough trying to write them, and only occasionally worrying that writing fiction was mere silly fantasy, a few unreal hours here and there, in Maine, on weekends and on vacation, travelling to worlds that I wasn't talented enough to display for others. Yet for the most part fiction did restore sanity. It patched me up just enough to bear more fisticuffs with the culture. A good novel made the plane to Dallas fly faster. In some glorious parole of retirement I would read and write and escape to my heart's content. But would it be enough? Maybe I did lose some brain cells of the creative and fictive kind (assuming I had any to start with). Maybe working hard for hard things (in the real world) takes the edge off your characters (in the story world). My hands and heart might be manacled, permanently. Am I free enough to escape?

Owls Head – its ocean, its woods, its ordinary lanes – slowly started to change me. Well before retirement, I started to write non-fiction as well, standard stuff like sketches of prairie desolation and college awakenings. The more I visited here in retirement, the more I got out of my head and into the facts and marvels of the natural world. This seems the right response to beauty. I came to realize that salvation for me lay not in creating a fictitious world of past or future but in seeing the glory and power and poetry of this one.

Rachael Carson, in her acceptance speech upon winning the National Book Award for her second book, *The Sea Around Us*, said, "The aim of science is to discover and illuminate truth. And that, I take it, is the aim of literature, whether biography or history or fiction. It seems to me, then, that there can be no separate literature of science. ... The winds, the sea, and the moving tides are what they are. If there is wonder and beauty and majesty in them, science will discover these qualities. If they are not there, science cannot create them. If there is poetry in my book about the sea, it is not because I deliberately put it there, but because no one could write truthfully about the sea and leave out the poetry."

After her career with US Fish and Wildlife Service, Carson began summering on Southport Island not too far from here. She made her living as a marine biologist, then a writer, and found a way to understand words through nature. She's an inspiration for someone like me trying the reverse course, someone who made a living from being an English major but who is finding a way to understand nature through words. We meet in the same place – the transformative coast of Maine.

****

I've walked the roads and lanes of Ash Point, our immediate neighborhood in Owls Head, hundreds or even thousands of times. When the family dog is in residence, she and I do only the mile-long loop – Bay View Terrace, Ash Point Drive, Canns Beach Road, Little Island Lane – and we do it clockwise in the morning, counterclockwise in the afternoon. When I'm alone, my daily walk goes farther and longer, on one of three routes, to Lucia Beach, to Crocketts Beach, or to Ash Point itself, trading them off each day like Hanukkah presents.

Lucia Beach Road stems off to the west from Ash Point Drive and follows the shore to that perfect pocket beach at its end. Every time I arrive there I stop for a few minutes, a little stunned, gazing at the handkerchief of sand, the big rocks standing in the surf, the ledge and fir trees promising another century in the state park just beyond, and the wonder lasts as long as I don't think too much about the houses crowding the shore.

And a new one is going up, huge as usual, filling its lot to the edges to ensure all manner of comfort within. I wouldn't have thought there was any building space left on Lucia Beach, but someone found a way. It doesn't look to be exactly on the water, but it's close enough for the owners to pretend.

Crocketts Beach Road lies north of us and leads to a shingle beach, one that has sand only at low tide. A public beach of a reasonable size is rare in this part of the world, and it's a popular place to sunbathe, and launch kayaks, and run dogs. By popular,

I mean that some hot days see as many as ten parked cars at once. When both wife and dog are in residence, and low tide coincides with the poodle's rigid walking schedule, we'll often walk there, for there's nothing Mia likes more. I find a stick and throw curveballs into the wind, and she proudly retrieves it, head high, ears blowing in the breeze. But soon the lure of treats is not enough. Soon she ignores the stick, and exhortations, and runs free, digging for clams and hopping on surf bubbles and pouncing on rolling sand grains as if they were alive. We laugh in delight. Making simple joys out of nothing, we all act like puppies again.

This part of the world has also had its brush with Hollywood. The movie "In the Bedroom" was shot in several places on the coast, including the cove behind Crocketts Beach, and during filming in 1999 or 2000 we walked there (just the once, mind you) to crane our necks. Sissy Spacek was rumored to be in the bus parked along the road. Todd Field the director actually lived in Owls Head for a while. As far as I know, the subsequent life of no resident was thereby transfigured.

The big house at the end of Crocketts Point is owned by someone I've recently met. He too is still officially from Massachusetts, but he's involved not only in a land trust, but in town government and County politics besides. He puts me to shame. He's someone who doesn't let his flatlandishness hold him back from acting like a local, in spite of what locals might say. Someday someone, in a fit of subtle Maine pique at his brashness at the annual town meeting, will remind him that the old name for his land is Shingle Belly Point.

The third walk goes down Ash Point Drive and ends in a town landing facing Ash Island. There's just enough space to park a car or two. The short way to get to the water is to clamber down a pile of bulldozed and broken concrete blocks, some state bureaucrat or out-of-town landowner's idea of progress, an ugly man-made mess if not for the beach roses and Muscle Ridge Islands growing all around. The occasional tourist comes, to park and drag his kayak down the longer track to the left, or to take a couple of minutes to enjoy the view before returning to the map and the road and the next peninsula. It is a lovely and pristine sight, elevated by the concrete, looking out on the bay, as long as you ignore the ranch house to the right, and the forlorn rusty utility pole and streetlight next to you, and on the left the large, plain Victorian farmhouse that used to announce itself grandly, in 3-foot letters, "Trails End," before the new owners took down that link to the past. As late as 1930, Trails End was the only house at the very end of Ash Point, now well represented by the well-to-do.

These three are my trinity of places, at which I never stop worshipping. Raspberries appear twice a year on Bay View Terrace, the second growth in September a gift of smallness and sweetness. On Lucia Beach Road I stop and look for the osprey nest; it can be seen only from a certain angle. I watch the slow browning of the leaves in fall, the sudden, spurting green of swamp cabbage in early spring. In election season opposing party signs often appear on lawns directly next to each other, and one lawn in the fall of 2012 boasted both a sign to re-elect a Republican and a sign to approve same-sex marriage. I see sea smoke in January, fog in July. Crows announce themselves any time, any place, but I have grown especially fond of the troop of seven or eight who inhabit our shore, and I look forward to what they have to say to me each day.

The variety of the same thing every day is redeemably amazing.

From each of these three land's ends – Lucia to the south, Crocketts to the north, Ash in the middle – it's possible to return home via the rocks and ledge and rockweed and tidal pools of the shore. I used to do so frequently, when time here was precious and I needed the solitude of open ocean to stretch it out. These days, however, are less desperate, and I'm not quite as spry; only under good conditions do I venture off the road and onto the rocks.

The shore from Crocketts to home is the easier one. I get to walk on sand (assuming low tide) for a quarter mile at pace, until the resumption of rocky terrain forces more care, hopping and balancing and progressing sideways as much as straightways. The houses here are built almost on top of the high-water mark, and the trespass I'm committing on intertidal property is obvious. The views are open, not so hemmed in by islands and points; the incline between land and sea is gradual like the bigger, more exploitable beaches farther south; and the cove is shallow and quiet and moors boats in the summer.

The walk from Ash Point going south to Lucia Beach (or of course north from Lucia Beach to Ash Point) presents a very different shorescape. It's a mile of rock and stones, a mile of frozen time, an incredible gamut of organized size and shape and style at which I, not being a geologist, can only wonder: first, a long stretch of rocks brain-sized and larger, owned by the unseen mansion on the bluff above; then, guarded by an immense boulder, a couple of hundred yards of gravel mixed with baseball-sized rocks, a poor man's beach for the six modest cottages built as close as possible, before the set-back laws took effect, to water; abruptly, rocks grow to cantaloupe size, a deep pile, and the houses grow as well, large and new and heavily taxed, banished from the edge; a thin tongue of granite next, trailed immediately by a beautiful house on a private cove whose rocks are small and washed in patterns as if anticipating a sand beach only a couple of million years in the future; followed by an expanse of classic Maine granite ledge, huge boulders slanting into the sea, scores of soft pinkish seats that demand a rest, views out to sea, poetics; finally, the white sand of Lucia's pocket beach, exquisitely held in arms of rock. This pattern is far beyond me – what combination of wind and wave formed these distinct sections? Is each composed of a consistent kind of rock, which then equally eroded? I don't understand this consistency, where every other shore I've seen seems a random jumble.

But when I start from Ash Point and walk north, that's when the archetypal Maine shore of slanting granite ledges, pointed fir trees, and surf appears. No houses: these 35 acres are owned by a man I've not yet met, who used to be prominent in the local land trust and who has protected his land under a conservation easement. *Down East* magazine could print this view and I for one would swear it's 200 miles north.

This shore is primeval and simple. The only signs of human presence are the lobster pots in the bay. The ospreys we see fishing in front of our house fly down this way with their catches and have their nest nearby, oddly enough not in these protected woods but in that tall tree on private land, near a driveway. I imagine deer (bear? moose? puma? saber-toothed tiger? why not?) walking along the trails at the edge of the bluff and venturing down now and then to drink from the pools of rainwater on the ledge. Walking out towards Ash Point from home, the kids and I discovered gorgeous tidal pools here a few years ago, full of primitive life like snails and crabs and pink starfish that we counted and named.

There's a bit of danger too, just as the illusion of wilderness should imply. I need to plan this walk for low tide, for high tide forces me up on steep boulders and ledges to get around some deep crevices, and I cling to bushes and dead trees to pass. The drop is only 15 or 20 feet, but the crevices are tricky, and the tide comes in fast, and dying in a wilderness only a few hundred yards from my house would be highly embarrassing. Only once have I given in to feeling old and scared, and I climbed up farther and walked the deer trails for a while, the country for old men.

Where the conservation land stops, the houses immediately begin, but I can't really see them. They are hidden by the bluff. I stop at the tide pools and worry about my daughters so far away. And then, at the end, there's nothing like climbing the little cliff at your own front lawn to give you a sense of place and commitment.

This is the walk I took obsessively in the fall of 2003 when I was spending time in Owls Head not necessarily by choice. That was the day in October when I came up from a crevice in the ledge, a small thunder hole where I had been standing for a while listening to the waves groan, and saw what I was always alert for. There was movement at the top of the bank, just at the edge of the bushes. Some small dark animal, so brown as to be nearly black, ventured out and immediately ducked into safety on seeing the human. Just an otter, I thought, rare enough at the ocean's edge. But it was too black, maybe it was a fisher cat. Whatever it was, it was rare and wild and it lived among us – wary of our dogs and development, not so casual with us as the deer and the fox to be sure, but here. And I had to sit down: all of it together – the islands, the surf, the fir trees, the fisher – brought tears to my eyes, tears of elation and longing and desperate worry about it all being taken away.

And that's why we obsess about houses on the waterfront. You think you can turn your back on your troubles. You believe you have arrived somewhere still and calm, where time and tide are the same. Look out in front of you, it's the illimitable ocean, you're safe, they can't get you here.

But of course they can. That October my life was changed for corporate reasons. I had been fired. And yet, even in a moment of despair, we are capable of beauty, seeing it and making it and losing it, and on that sparkling day, in my second week of unemployment, I made sure to touch one foot to the sand of Lucia Beach, just to make a mark before the tide came in, to complete a circle, to bond with tides, to over-ride the toxins of life, grateful at least for one chelating moment in time.

****

In the 19th century Ash Point was an actual village, with a church, a school that doubled as a dance hall, and a general store. It used to be overgrown with ash trees. A fishing weir extended

125

between the point and the island. Its inhabitants descended from the people given land in this area for services rendered in 1776 – Heard, Packard, Crockett.

Almost all of "my" familiar shore, from Crocketts Point to Lucia Beach, was at one time owned by Crocketts. There are still Crocketts in our neighborhood, although Charlie, the last male, died in early 2012. His wife lives on in the brown house they occupied their whole lives; his only child, a daughter, lives a hundred yards away, just up the hill, in plain sight; two of his grandchildren also live in houses on the "compound"; and two female cousins reside nearby. Our own deed has an easement on it from nearly a hundred years ago: Eliza M. Crockett and her heirs and assigns have the right to walk on the intertidal zone in front of our house. Not that they would, not that they have much to do with us at all, or more accurately, it's us who don't have much to do with them, not even knowing who they are, or if any still live here, or live at all.

It's only now that I'm getting to know a few people in this town, it's only recently (a blustery day in March), that I explored Ash Point Cemetery, making a start with the dead people, as if were, and only now, after 17 years of coming and going, that I'm feeling more acutely that I've been not much more than a tourist.

The cemetery has a metal arch over one entrance with the dates 1820 – 1939. I don't know what the dates mean. Interrogation of impersonal sources tells me nothing. The dates don't mean that the cemetery was closed in 1940, for I've seen several fresh graves, and once the aftermath of a burial, people standing around in the Maine casual way, no suits or long faces, smiling and joking, as I walked by. I've walked by thousands of times but for once, I'm actually in amongst the graves.

There are a couple of hundred headstones, and every name on them is English except one that's French, one that's Finnish, and one that ends in "z." There's a curious modesty about the stones. The old ones have their backs to the road, and I have to go around them to see names and dates. And at the very back of the cemetery, the fence is so close to the stones that I have to squeeze in to get a look. But then I look up and over. Of course: these folks would want their visitors to face in the direction of the ocean, so long the source of collective livelihoods, as they remembered the past.

The newer monuments are bigger and not so self-effacing. Their names and dates face the road for all to see, a drive-by advertisement for the self and not the life. I wonder in which decade the attitude began to change.

At least two dozen stones are marked Crockett. They stand mostly in family groups, in three of the four corners of the cemetery, exceeded in size and number only by the stones of Hurd/Heard occupying the middle territory: the uptown and downtown of Owls Head, if you will. I sense some kind of ancient feud.

I look for Eliza. She lies under three markers. Eliza D. (Crowell) Crockett lived from 1816 to 1899. At her feet a simple piece of polished granite, marking what was undoubtedly a daughter, says only "Eliza." A third stone some yards away records "Eliza Crockett, 1846-1925." This Eliza could be the one mentioned on our deed (although the lack of that middle initial "M" argues against it), for our house, then just a cottage, was erected in 1924. Even if she isn't the one, the fantasy is rich: all the houses here were once cottages (only a couple still occupy their original footprints), built by Crocketts for their descendants or for income, and some have an easement similar to ours, and I like the idea of an old woman in her 70s, walking down the shore to check on the housekeeping habits of a daughter-in-law. Of course, knowing which Eliza wanted the right to walk the shore really makes no difference to me. What may make a difference is how the Crocketts still living here feel about the place, how they relate to the land, and others taking it over. I'm no genealogical maniac, gaining satisfaction in some Ellis Island of the mind, and when I get up the nerve to ask my neighbors, I'm quite prepared to have fantasy bubbles burst. The truth can be

127

mundane, i.e., nobody knows, as well as exotic. This perpetual re-visitor would be pleased just to have any connection at all to the stalwarts of this place.

Charlie Crockett is not buried in Ash Point Cemetery. It is full, or fully reserved; indeed, a couple of years ago the town claimed some land near the airport (alas, a blueberry field much beloved by my daughters and me) as a new town cemetery. Yet Charlie decided to be buried not there, but in Rockland. Perhaps he couldn't stand to repeat in eternal rest what he suffered in life – to be directly under a flight path serving Knox County Regional Airport. But in his honor and to cement his place in Owls Head, the family made kind of a local memorial. Just up the hill from his house, on a large stone, a so-called erratic carried by glaciers from somewhere else, they have carved the name "Crockett," incisively, eternally. It rests half on the lawn that he was so particular about, half in a field of lupine, that wildest and most ordinary of flowers. The irony is deep and painful: the rock is a memorial to all the shore land the Crocketts once owned, a way of remembering the Crockett name when Nancy too will die and the house that sits practically on the rocks of the shore will be sold to someone from somewhere else. The druid stone sits solid, a counterpoint to the life increasingly restless and erratic around it.

Charlie's granddaughter now takes care of the lawns, riding the lawn mower with Charlie's great-grandson on her lap, just as assiduously as ever he did. Charlie's son-in-law is building a third house, for the last granddaughter. Forever may the Crocketts see the lupine in the field, and the great purple lilac bushes of an eternal spring, and the powerful ocean on the edge of the parlor, and if they must leave and can't see them anymore, then the rock will remember.

Ash Point has changed, like everything does. There is no community left, only houses now. No dances at the schoolhouse, no gatherings at the store. Most mornings it's like a ghost town, deserted as a cemetery – the little houses mostly owned by old people who stay inside, the big houses mostly owned by flatlanders who are seldom there. The major activity seems to be remodeling – making the small houses bigger, and adding great rooms and sun rooms and granite kitchen countertops to those that are already mansions. What is it like for a Crockett to live in such a changed place, where most of your remaining connections to land lie in the graveyard? In the opposite case, what would it be like for me to have connections here? Would Owls Head become a home as well as a sanctuary?

****

A colleague told me, to my face but laughing, in a land trust meeting in which I introduced myself to a guest as a half-Mainer, "You'll never be a Mainer." She meant it in the nicest possible way, I'm sure, she being one. Is it that obvious, I said to myself, as chagrin led to slight depression.

I know I can be foolish about my passion for this place, Maine in general and Owls Head in particular. I proselytize for it, my inner John Calvin peeking out, although I try to keep him gentle; I preach salvation not by hellfire and damnation but by rockweed and bird song. But my big fear is that I'll always be a visitor, or at best a re-visitor. This can be said, of course, of anyone who lives on this earth, even those whose ancestors stretch to the Puritans on the Mayflower, or *Homo habilis* in Olduvai Gorge for that matter, for we all seek a better home and won't find it.

And yet...and yet. There's something about this place that transcends the fear of death (aka, the uncertainty of heaven).

What have I learned in nearly 30 years of driving back and forth on the Maine Turnpike?

Familiarity. I love walking and seeing the same things at different times, in different lights, in different seasons. I love walking up ordinary Bay View Terrace (especially now that my neighbors repaired it in a most enlightened way – by removing the asphalt in favor of plain, old-fashioned dirt): the crystalline air; the birches and evergreens and red winterberries; moss-covered stones, green as tropical atolls in all seasons; the ferns of April and the sex-filled insistent thrill of the peepers of May; summer's raspberries and blackberries and impenetrable vegetation; under the spruce boughs snow drifts never broken by plow or boot; fifteen kinds of mushrooms if you look hard enough; the astonishment of purple flowers; the hope of seeing deer and fox at any moment. Staring at the ocean puts me in a deep trance of love. Every day I wake to look out the window and praise the pointed fir tree on the edge of the bank, literally on the edge, trunk splitting upwards with the strain of hanging on, yet which has doubled in size since we moved here. One day it will crash into the ocean, to die at its peak striving for life. I want to be here to see that, to grieve and celebrate at the same time.

A familiar sense of place (it doesn't have to be this place, but the ocean shore particularly suits my eschatology) is crucial to repair lifetimes spent driving and jetting and selling. I, for one, lived in more than 30 different houses before settling down to my current two. Progress!

The shore. The shore makes me think of creation and life, death and resurrection (all of which may be, at this point of my thinking, but a matter of molecules). It is the intersection between worlds. John O'Donohue in his mystical book *Anam Cara: A Book of Celtic Wisdom* says, "for millions of years, an ancient conversation has continued between the chorus of the ocean and the silence of the stone." I hear those echoes, but also sense the unheard – the incredible fecundity of the inter-tidal zone, the trillions of plankton and barnacles and algae and mollusks and fish, not to mention the uncountable number of their seeds. How can one, like Rachel Carson, not fall in love with every step? Walking on the shore, I seem to be tied to the moment of creation, whether that creation takes a second, a lifetime, or 4.5 billion years.

Solitude. For me, a familiar place has to be rural. The shore has chosen me, but for others the woods, the plains, the mountains could be equally rewarding. The important thing is to connect with something bigger than yourself, to be outside of the ego, to eschew the works of humans at regular intervals, to make it impossible to turn too far inward. John O'Donohue again: "Solitude is one of the most precious things in the human spirit. It is different from loneliness. When you are lonely, you become acutely conscious of your own separation. Solitude can be a homecoming to your own deepest belonging."

The feeling of coming home, being home, is crucial not only to well-being but also to creative acts. Examining the world requires being solitary in it. Paradoxically, the press of people turns my thoughts too far inward. But solitude also implies, at least to me, the other kind of homecoming – that you must return to family and friends and the social side of being human. Getting the balance right is the challenge. I try to remember that even hermit crabs change their shells when they grow up, and so revisitation drives me back south as well as up north.

What's worse than being a hermit? Being addicted to "social" (ha!) media. The loneliness of people oppressed by the city is a tragedy beyond comprehension.

People. I've found a place to lie down and rest, and I hope to convey a little of that peace to others. The bigger problems for Earth remain unsolved, however, and the solution (I'm trying to convince myself) is a human one as much as a natural one. We've reached, and probably have exceeded, the carrying capacity of this Earth. There are too many of us, or too many of us want all the things that the lucky few of us have. And so the paradoxes of 21st century life overwhelm me. I don't have too much trouble understanding the natural conversations, but human ones, well, there's where I fall down.

Little Island Lane

****

As I stand at the end of Ash Point, looking out on the bay, there are no people in view, just a few score hidden in the nearby houses, just a few billion hidden by the earth's curvature and willful disregard. Ironically, I feel the human drama much more acutely on the shore than in the city. I see the ghosts of Native Americans. I see European adventurers: this area became the de facto dividing line between the French colonists and priests to the north (and their battle for the hearts and minds of the Abenaki) and the British colonists and ministers to the south (and their battle for the land and riches of the Abenaki). Then I see the terrible cost of independence, as both sides merged and became the mercenary missionaries so peculiar to the American continent. Humans have acted this way – territorial, aggressive, consuming – for thousands of years, and the shore, ever-changing but always the same, is a sharp rebuke. The city changes and is never the same – that's a rebuke as well. Importunities assault me in the city, so much so that they become mere deadening noise, and my first reaction to almost every opportunity or emotion is "no." I hardly see the works of God in the city at all.

In the city, people seem perpetually afraid. I quote a London gravestone: "Here lies Jeremy Brown, born a man, died a grocer." Even a king, for all the beauty and strength of his castle, is ruled mostly by fear, and he thinks armor is needed out there among the grocers beyond the moat. On the shore, in the woods, I put it that people can think more carefully and lovingly and empathetically. Here, I hope that we can sense all of life and death together – plankton, rockweed, peeky-toe crab, seagull, fisher cat, human – as we die and dry and fly away, struggling against it yet at last accepting. Acceptance is not really allowed in the city, often not even in the family. One must compete – not accede – to survive. In the city you may be seduced into thinking you have control; the tides and the storms of the ocean make that wish seem silly. The shore and the forests and the mountains enfold humans, put us in our place, and make us seek God not as a solution to the suffering of civilization but as an eminence in all.

But in the city I get most of my human contacts: dinners with friends, book group discussions, reading aloud with neighbors, block parties. It's a community – do I need another? Set this against what amounts to date as a hermit's life in Owls Head, where the great majority of my society consists of the committee and board meetings of a land trust, unless you count librarians, the guys at the dump, and the clerks at the supermarket. Is yet another investment worth it?

Clearly, I haven't figured out the benefits and costs of a new life. Clearly, I may never. There might be no grand solution. I was taught in my youth that there will be and must be one (Calvinism – you don't want to know the details), and that may be the problem – and not only for me. It seems to me that final solutions tend to be bloody, so a meek person will shy away from pursuing despots and preachers and importuners of all kinds. People like me are mostly content to watch Nature, and recount and report its glories for others. Thoreau wrote in his Journal for March 15, 1852: "I am eager to report the glory of the universe; may I be worthy to do it; to have got through with regarding human values, so as not to be distracted from regarding divine values."

That's not to say I shouldn't do more, and be rewarded therefrom. My fellow travelers here in Maine have much to tell and teach me. There are many people to get to know better, activists and farmers, neighbors, donors, Crocketts and Heards. Writers and artists and musicians are thick on the ground. The culture is intimate, not striving. Maine appeals so much to people like me because it mitigates, through the beauty of the land and the tolerance of the people, the reality that we're ultimately alone. People migrate here with an incredible variety of experiences, a brimming sense of responsibility, a burning need to love something. Bob Rheault, the man who donated his shoreline acres to a land trust? I finally meet him. He's old and sits at a desk doing paperwork and talks about saving land and I know from Google he commanded all Special Forces during the Vietnam War.

People like Bob and me won't ever be Mainers, but Maine makes the terrible reality of ultimate loneliness tolerable, enjoyable, even necessary.

****

You may be wondering why I don't just give in to heritage and tradition and go all Christian on you – for example, follow John O'Donohue into his claims about the soul as well as the stone. I seem to fit the type, naïve that way. But it's impossible. I just don't have it. When pursued to the end of logic, religious people have to admit that the only evidence of God is emotional, some kind of touch, some kind of deep feeling granted, not earned. Thinking won't get you there – the contradictions of good and evil are too immense. So I look for something else to make it through.

Charles Ryder in *Brideshead Revisited* tried it all – friendship, marriage, tradition, adultery, career, religion. He visited and revisited and at the end, he could not capture a place of dreams, he never did arrive anywhere, he was ultimately unsatisfied, and had to turn to God. Had he been touched, or did he settle in the face of despair? His conversion seems tenuous and bland to me. Perhaps his life was fatally swayed, attracted to the wrong people for the wrong reasons, and thus doomed by the inevitable restlessness of Ryders and inconstancy of Flytes. For whatever reason, I was never swept up in great piles of romantic love and forgiving church and loving community and crumbling ancestral mansions. At best I've discovered that salvation is a place where one belongs, with work one must do, and I hope to understand how people and tradition might fit.

Unfortunately, my temptation is to hide away, and this often creates a rift. Healing the rift will involve people and tradition, something a little frightening after being so much in the built world by necessity and not by nature. Part of this is the rural aspect, or perhaps the difference between a fact-based ethos and a faith-based one. One seems to need faith and fiction to survive in the city, one needs to be both missionary and pagan.

I'm not envious of those with belief. After all, how much does one miss by thinking all the time of Heaven?

For the post-religious or the irreligious, what can we do but trust the stories of our eyes and receive their touch of immortality? For me the stories of the world unfold in a small town in coastal Maine. The natural stories here can stand for the whole universe as far as I'm concerned. I need hardly leave my neighborhood (the lure of California, Scotland, Paris notwithstanding!) to be awed as much as any Christian in a cathedral. But the human stories also need attention. The great majority of people seem to think so, darn them.

I expect to travel between city and country, people and nature, for some years to come, but such is a journey between good and better. This may mean that the shape of this third life, after a first one of unlearning Calvinism, and a second of unlearning corporate-ism, will be ill-defined for a while. What ism must I unlearn next? Or will I actually learn something, like how to find community? Will revisitation become a matter of connecting with people as much as with nature? Of learning there is no end.

It also could be that there's nothing more to believe in; after all, we are indeed ultimately alone. All I really know is that I live and die for my daily walks in Owls Head. That's where I can best find a context for living, and experience life's greatest ironies – that getting involved in something so deeply means you forget self-consciousness, that re-creating that feeling uses words that are always imperfect and may never be read. And if your immortality lasts through history, or only for a generation of surnames, or in an essay, or for a minute on the shore, who's to parse the difference?

****

I try to imagine the last walk I'll take in Owls Head. Maybe it's just a few yards along Little Island Lane, as our 90-year-old neighbors do. Maybe I'll be accompanied by wife, daughter, friend, paid attendant. The air will be sweet, the trees will crouch around me, the leaves and needles under my feet will be pungent with decay. A strong arm supports me, or a cane, a walker, a wheelchair. Afterwards, someone will put me in a chair on the deck, wrapped against the chill fall breeze. The ocean will know me, its surf will wave goodbye.

Then again, I probably won't know it's a last walk. The very next day could bring an accident, or a stroke. If it's all the same to you, I'd rather not know, for I expect hope to spring eternal. I'll forever expect to walk again tomorrow. And if I don't, I hope that the moment of death will be a last visit to the shore, a moment of great revelation and a meeting with my soul, as the mystics say, when all the mysteries of the world are revealed and my molecules fly away to join everything else and I see all of time at once. Probably that won't be true. But until I find out, I will look for my moments of joy and sorrow in a wave from a neighbor, a fox on the lawn, a memory of lanes, sunrise over the islands, in a place that passes all understanding.

About the Author

Jim Krosschell divides his time between Owls Head, Maine and Newton, Massachusetts. After a career in science publishing in the Boston area, he began writing much more regularly, and more than 50 journals and magazines have published his personal essays (and versions of several of the chapters herein). Besides writing and contributing to the welfare of the Maine Turnpike, he is also president of the Board of Directors, Coastal Mountains Land Trust, in Camden, Maine.

www.ingramcontent.com/pod-product-compliance
Lightning Source LLC
Chambersburg PA
CBHW031135090426
42738CB00008B/1093